Love's Quiet Revolution

SCOTT KILOBY

The End
of the
Spiritual
Search

ISBN: 1-4196-9578-9
ISBN-13: 9781419695780

To Mom, Dad, and Family for the support

To Mark F. for being compassion when the phone rang

To Kenny M. for igniting the fire

To Kevin P. & Tom M. for meeting me in the truth

To Chad for being love

Contents

Prologue

To be, without divisions, is love

Despite its fancy words, this book is conveying a very simple message of pure love. It was written in the months after an awakening into Oneness, which is a spiritual transformation that is difficult to put into words. The sense of being a separate self died in that transformation, leaving an inexplicable love for the whole of life. This book is a set of reflections or insights that were revealed in that awakening.

There is a revolution happening on earth right now. You will not hear guns, bombs, and breaking news alerts on CNN during this revolution. This is an inward, quiet revolution of the spirit. Love is devouring the separation, conflict, and war of this illusion we call the human ego. This book points to that spiritual transformation. It points to a liberation that cannot be named with any mental certainty. Yet it can be known and experienced undoubtedly as your very presence. Throughout this book, I use the words "This," "One," "Oneness," "consciousness," "God," "presence," "truth," "enlightenment," "beingness," "love," "spirit," and "liberation" interchangeably to point to that freedom. This freedom is not in the words. It is not found through belief or through emphasizing thoughts about yourself, others, the world, or anything else. Freedom is not something that can be neatly packaged into a concept. It is not something to believe and it is not something that can be summed up in a sentence or statement. The freedom being pointed to in this book is freedom from any fixed conceptions of reality, freedom from believing that your thoughts are delivering absolute truth. It is freedom from believing that truth can be found in a fleeting concept. And all concepts are fleeting. It is freedom from believing that your identity can be found or located in thought. All concepts are seen to come and go within a timeless presence. That presence is where true freedom naturally resides. You cannot reach this presence in time. It is what is looking at these words right now. How can you find what is looking right now in some future moment? And how can you find what is looking right now in just one concept or even a set of concepts appearing in this book. All concepts are temporarily appearing and disappearing within what is presently looking. Realizing that is freedom. That is enlightenment. If you recognize, not intellectually, but with your whole being, what is being pointed to in this paragraph, there is no reason to read the rest of the book. You have realized this freedom.

I prefer the word 'This' as a pointer and use it repeatedly throughout the book. The word 'This' points to life itself, not some future dream of enlightenment or esoteric idea or belief system. 'This' is completely accessible as who you truly are in this moment. The word 'This' is preferred simply because it does not carry the same degree of cultural, historical, and religious baggage as the words "God," "enlightenment," and others listed above. The word 'This' points to Oneness, which means to the realization that no thing is separate from any other thing. Another word for the freedom talked about in this book is "non-duality." Non-duality means "not two." Non-dual realization is a seeing that there are no separate things in life, despite what thought tells us. Separation (e.g., between you, me, this, and that) is a product of thought. It is a belief system.

As humans, we believe our thoughts, every one of them. And thoughts, when they arise within the mind, seem to point to separate things out there in the world. If the thought "tree" arises, we believe there is such a thing as a tree, existing separately from the rest of the universe. Non-duality, then, is the seeing through of that separation. It is actually possible in this lifetime to realize that separation is illusory, that everything is inseparable from everything else. When that realization dawns upon you, freedom is seen to be your very nature. You are free of the belief in separation and the suffering, conflict, and seeking that comes with it. So enlightenment, you, presence, soccer, dogs, buildings, your neighbor, humility, pencils, religion, thought, love, water bottles, liberation, bananas, lamps, cars, clouds, and moons constitute one inseparable life that I call 'This.' Thought will never grasp any of that because thought is responsible for fragmenting 'This' into all these words that create the illusion of separateness. Yet, once 'This' is seen, it is realized as undeniably true.

This ultimate truth must—and does—include all the major religions, including the ones that profess that there is a central deity, as well as those that point to some state of human transcendence or enlightenment without a central deity. At the heart of each religion is one light of truth. This book merely points to that light. That light is freedom from the belief in separation. This light is the end of all suffering and seeking. More pointedly, the realization of this light within shows you that all suffering is a dream, and therefore it never began. To make this book solely about Hinduism, Christianity, Buddhism or any other religion, tradition, practice, or method would be to fragment the one truth to which the book points.

As I said, the basic message of the book is love. True love simply does not see any fragmentation. It sees and loves the whole because it is the whole looking at itself. In a way that the mind cannot grasp, the truth includes and celebrates all these religions, traditions, practices, and methods. Oneness excludes nothing. It is everything.

If you are reading this book and are turned off by the "spiritual" language in it, look again. This is a book about life. Humans are spiritual seekers. Spiritual seeking is the movement towards the future, emanating from a sense of lack or incompleteness. Each of us carries that lack within. This book is about the evaporation of that sense of lack. So this book is not a spiritual book at all. It is a celebration of life itself. It points to the seeing that this moment contains perfect completeness. This book applies, then, to anyone who reads it. To be human is to be a search. This book is about seeing through, and therefore, ending that search.

If you finish this book having added a new belief system, the point of the book has been missed. More than anything, it is an invitation to stop believing that we know how life really is. In the free-fall of not knowing, all lines of division within the mind are seen through. What is left is not a belief system or mental position. It is so free that the intellect cannot capture it by name. Love is as good a word as any.

The Search Named "Scott"

I see no separate "me" here. I see no separate "you" there. I see no separate things. The word "I" is used only for communication purposes. It would be impossible to write a book without words. But the fact that there are words in this book does not mean that the words are pointing to separate objects.

There was once a time-based, mind-made story named "Scott," and such past conditioning comes through now and again. But "Scott" was a spiritual search, a dream. I still turn my head when someone in the room says my name. I still put my name on tax forms. I can still tell you all the details of the memories of childhood, and the years before and after this dream event called "the awakening" (except for the details that drugs erased).

I am reluctantly providing details of the story of Scott, not because the past is painful to think or talk about now, but rather because I no longer identify with it. There is no "me" here to identify with the dream of thought known as "past." So, I lose interest very quickly while talking about the dream of "Scott," and "his past." The past rarely surfaces anymore. When it does, it is seen as only presently arising thoughts to which there is no attachment. Nonetheless, I will share some of the details of this spiritual search named "Scott" in case you are interested in the story.

I grew up in a small town in Indiana in an upper middle class family. My wonderful parents showered me with love, attention, and material things. I was a fairly happy young child, albeit a spoiled brat. I was given anything I wanted or requested. I do not blame my parents for my being a spoiled brat. I was hardwired with a sense of lack and an insatiable appetite for more.

I was a shy kid who needed attention. I wanted to be somebody special in the eyes of others, but at the same time I wanted to be left alone. This dualism created quite a tug of war in me throughout my childhood and teenage years. A performer at heart, I loved dancing, putting on puppet shows, lip syncing to music, entertaining the neighborhood kids with homemade haunted houses and challenging kids on the block to races and athletic events. I was called "a natural athlete" while growing up, excelling in just about every sport I tried. Sports kept me out of trouble. But ultimately, the success and attention I achieved in sports did not fulfill the deep desire in me to be somebody or find whatever I was seeking.

An extremely sensitive child, I fell apart emotionally and mentally when anyone criticized or poked fun at me. This sensitivity left me afraid of people and most social situations. I was bullied in grade school. The pain and fear led me to look for escape mechanisms. I tried marijuana for the first time at age twelve. By age fourteen, marijuana had become my favorite method of escape. When I was high, the entire world fell away. At age fourteen, I began playing guitar and writing songs. This too was a way to avoid what felt like a very confusing world "out there." I spent hours upon hours in my room, alone, writing music and playing. I lived in my own fantasy land.

Through the years, I was labeled by fellow musicians, friends, and family members as a "gifted songwriter." This provided just the right amount of ego food for my insecurity. Except for the times when I was writing, performing or playing sports, however, I never knew quite how to fit into my own skin. I learned early in life to put on a good front and wear the mask of comfortableness.

The older I got, the more isolated I felt socially. I was "self-conscious" as they say, always hesitating before acting, watching to see who was watching me and what others were thinking about me. I began to feel increasingly insatiable and lost through my high school and college years. I felt like an alien. There was this constant nagging feeling inside that I had somehow landed on the wrong planet, that nothing here would ever be good enough, and that total acceptance of myself and life would always be out of reach.

No matter what was given to me in terms of material items, love, attention, or success, it did not fill the void. It was difficult for me to truly appreciate anything. I always wanted more, better, and different. At the core, I felt less than, not better, and different. The alienation, restlessness, and sensitivity led to increased drug use. By age twenty, I had become a full-blown drug addict. I lived in active addiction for several years. There were times when I enjoyed life. Drugs were often a playground, a way to escape into another world. During short periods of clean time, I would be somewhat engaged in life, relationships, and work. But no matter what happened, there was an underlying sense of restlessness and dissatisfaction with life. This led to more and more drug use and desperation.

I played in rock bands throughout my teens and twenties. More than anything else, I was seeking validation and love. I was looking for the end of the dissatisfaction and believed that if millions of people loved my music, I would find what I was seeking. Although the music career hinted at success, it ultimately crashed in my twenties, due largely to addiction.

I went through one failed relationship after another in my twenties, never finding the love for which I was longing. I seemed to pick the wrong people, those who would not or could not reciprocate my feelings. I could not find that right person, and when I found someone who I believed could fulfill that need, I fell so deeply in love that it would turn to obsession and jealousy, driving the person away. When someone would become interested in me romantically, and would chase or court me, I would push them away. I was much more interested in searching than finding. I repeated this self-defeating behavior over and over. I spent years trying to heal deep wounds from these relationships.

I hit bottom after years of drug use and ended up in a twelve-step program. The program was exactly what I needed to help me stay clean and sober, but I continued searching in recovery for meaning and purpose for my life. I read book after book about how to find happiness. I had lived a life of always wanting the next moment to happen, and never feeling satisfied with anything. I never got "there" but I didn't know what "there" would look like if it were "here." I wanted more, and when I got more, that was not enough. So the spiritual seeking was no different than the drug using. It was all a search. I was a junkie—the drug had changed from material items, to success in sports, to marijuana, to songwriting and fame-seeking, to painkillers, to spirituality. In those first few years of recovery, I went through just about every religion and spiritual method, looking for my freedom. I was looking for myself.

The Awakening

During the spiritual search, I discovered certain nondual teachings. I saw that these teachers were pointing to real freedom. Not freedom that comforts the ego but a freedom that obliterates it. A freedom that leaves you nothing to stand on. It leaves no "you." It leaves only love. Nonduality. Non-separation. Whatever you want to call it.

While reading these books, I began to notice every thought and emotion that arose in each moment. I was not looking for enlightenment. I just wanted the alienation, dissatisfaction, and restlessness to end.

I remember the first "shift" well. On a cold February afternoon, I was driving in my car, and all of a sudden the sense of being rigidly separate from the rest of life melted away. For two weeks after that experience, I felt a very intense, pleasurable ball of tightly-wound energy in my chest. I did not know what was happening and had no name for this build-up of energy. I am sure there is some enlightenment term for it. But I had an intuitive sense that I was in the middle of some shift in consciousness.

At the end of that two weeks, I found myself sitting on my bed on a Saturday night. Peace flooded through my whole body and mind from the inside out. It took me over. My mind quieted. I realized that there was truly stillness "out there" in the room, and in the world, and that this same stillness was within me, as who I really am. The ball of energy stayed in my chest until the next day when I was watching *Grey's Anatomy* (one of my favorite shows). In this episode, a lady was giving birth, and at the same time, in some other place, her husband was dying. I began crying, sobbing. In some way that is hard to explain, I was not crying for her. I was seeing clearly in that moment the impermanence of life. It was not a thought. I did not think, "Life is impermanent." I saw and felt it with my whole being.

The next morning, as I walked to work, something was very different. I was now looking at life from within the awareness in the body, from the stomach and chest area, rather than through the processor of the mind. It was as if my heart was now connecting directly with everything my eyes saw, and that this seeing bypassed the filter of thought. This was clearly a shift in consciousness. It felt as though the universe had downloaded insight into my being. I saw clearly that all of the divisions, religions, methods, practices, nations, and groups were the result of the fragmentation of the mind. Outside of thought, no such fragmentation exists. I saw and felt that the history of suffering of humanity in wars, inquisitions, the holocaust, genocide, drugs, violence, abuse, oppression and religious and political conflict resulted from one fundamental misunderstanding: the idea of a separate self. Consciousness is entangled in these false, divisive thought structures. These thought-based divisions were seen as part of a dream of separation that obscures the spirit—the truth of who we are.

I knew this was not a final awakening though. I could not put my finger on it. But I could just tell that this "wasn't it." For the next few months, I lived in what can only be described as deep inner peace, but there was still a very subtle seeking energy right on the surface of my being. There was still a "Scott" searching for something, as if the deeper and final truth was right around the corner.

About five months later, I was driving home on a warm July evening after sitting for hours around a campfire with friends from a twelve-step fellowship, roasting marshmallows and discussing politics and religion. I felt what can only be described as little sparks firing all through my body—little explosions, one after the other, from head to toe. Thought slowed down. A sense of clarity seemed to arise from the slowing of thought. I was becoming more and more alert and attentive to my surroundings, to the space in my inner body, to the road, to everything.

When I got home, I jumped up on my bed. I was lying on my back, with one hand on each of my dogs, Josie and Mai-Ling. As I petted the dogs, a thought arose: "Consciousness just wants to see itself." The sparks started firing again. I suddenly knew that I was not petting my dogs. I realized they were not separate from me.

I stood up, and walked around my apartment, completely stunned at what I was seeing. I was seeing the nature of reality beyond thought. I was seeing that there was no me separate from any "thing" I was looking at. It feels strange now to use subject/object language to describe the complete absence of separation. All thought stopped—completely. I saw myself as the floor, the wall, the desk, the window, the streetlight outside, and in everything else upon which these eyes fell. I found myself on the floor, grabbing at the carpet, and laughing my head off. I laughed, and laughed, and laughed. I kept saying fervently, "None of this matters, none of this matters!" You may ask, "What didn't matter?" My only answer is that it was clear that "nothing mattered," at least not in the way I had always thought. The search, the lack, the dissatisfaction, the fear, the anger, the resentment did not matter. It was all seen as a dream of self-centeredness.

I realized that I cannot find myself because there is no self. I saw that I am what I had been seeking. But when I say "I am," I mean the One, whatever that means. There was no Scott experiencing any of this. There was only the experiencing. 'This' was seeing itself. It was clear that whatever this word God is pointing to, it is right here, now. It is, and always was, right under my nose, as my nose, and everything on each side of it, behind it, inside it, and over it. The notion of seeking God was seen as pointless. It was realized that there is only 'This' and that nothing is separate from it.

The only thing that remained as the laughter released the dream of "Scott" was brilliant, loving space. This space was alive, fully alive and radiant. The miracle and mystery of life was seen for the first time, yet it had always been here. I had just been too busy looking for it, looking for some dream of future that thought had created. It was clear that nothing was separate from anything else, and that only thought created separateness. I remember saying, "All this time, I thought I was a person named 'Scott' living on the second floor of this apartment. What a joke!"

I remember staring at a digital clock by the bed and laughing hysterically at the notion that this One— whatever it is—would even bother with the concept of time. There is only ever 'This,' outside of time. I noticed that wherever I moved, whatever area of the apartment I moved into, I was still only ever in 'This.' I was 'This.' I could not leave. Where was I going to go? I saw clearly that we do not die, not in the way we think we do. We simply move into a different energy form. I remember uttering the words, "We don't die, we don't die" over and over. This was not a belief that was being formed. It was not a memory of something said by some guru in a book. It was a realization beyond belief. Literally. I saw that it could only have been realized in the absence of thought and belief. I saw that reality can only be seen in the absence of thought and belief. My fear of death left in that moment, as did my fear of life. "Scott" as a thought-based self simply vanished. The search was over. Nothing to seek. Nothing, nothing. 'This' is all there is, and it is so perfectly enough.

In the Wake of the Dream

What has been left in the wake of the dream is difficult to put into words. "Love" is a good description. However, 'This' is a very different kind of love. It is not the attached love of the dream state. This love is a love for the whole of life. It is unconditional. This love devoured the "me" and all its conditions. Whatever one may call 'This,' it feels deeply liberated from caring about what it is called. In the two weeks after the awakening, I found myself buying a webcam and recording one video message after another, speaking—without any notion of a need for a script or editing—about this awakening and what had been left in its aftermath. In truth, nothing had been left. The past was gone. There was only peace, love, joy, awareness, emptiness. And even those are just words. There was a profoundly deep realization that no words or thoughts can touch the ultimate truth. At the same time, 'This' just wanted to express itself through words. I created hours of videos in those two weeks, all in some attempt to communicate this inexpressible love.

In the next few months, I created the website www. kiloby.com. I placed many of those first videos on the site. It seems funny to even use the word "I" here because there was no sense of a self doing anything, or trying to achieve any result. The chapters in this book were written during the six months after the awakening. The world of form was somehow coming back into 'This' to be included. Some formless reality wanted to be expressed through form, so to speak. As nutty as this may sound to the mind, this reality was expressing itself through me. And this is the great paradox that can never really be expressed about non-dual realization. There are no separate things, yet there is the appearance of separate things. There is no Scott, yet Scott appears, like a conceptual dream, like an illusion that has no solid, independent, "real" existence. It's an illusion that appears to write a book, just as there is the illusion of a reader of this book. Yet, they are "not two." Subject and object arise together, seamlessly, inseparably, out of nothing.

Non-duality means "not two." Somehow, those two "seeings" (of nothing being everything) are not inconsistent at all. If this were only about holding one view, if this were only about nothing existing, or only about everything existing separately, that wouldn't be non-duality at all. It would be just another dualistic viewpoint. Non-duality is not about finding a new viewpoint about "the way things really are." It is about challenging everything you think you know about the "way things really are." What is left is absolute liberation.

After the Oneness experience described above, I suppose I could have gone to a monastery, meditating quietly for years in pure formless awareness. But I did not, and so my busy life as an attorney continued moving. After the awakening, I went to work on Monday morning just like any other week. But something was drastically different. There was no longer a concept of "me" or "attorney" or "job" or "work" or "career." Work was no longer a chore. "Chore" was seen as an illusory concept. There was only this moment—footsteps to the office, arms moving to grab papers, fingers moving to type briefs, walking to courthouse, arguments made to judges. Joy. Love. No problems. No self. No center. No more spiritual search. No effort. Life turned from a noun to a verb, so to speak. Instead of Scott, work, lunch, problems, friends, people, clients, cases, day, week, month, and life, it became living, doing, moving, loving, touching, tasting, feeling, and being in this moment. Life was living itself through this body and mind.

This body and mind began to embody the One in a way that is difficult to describe. 'This' was coming back for the whole truth, including a heightened awareness of the simple facts of everyday humanness: the little moments in life such as the dogs running by, the sound of coffee pouring into a cup, the wind on my face, the sensation of a headache, the feeling of an elbow on the desk, the smile or frown on a friend's face, and the vast space embracing everything. There was also a heightened awareness of the illusory suffering around me: the clients arguing with one another, the family members struggling with this or that mind-created problem, and friends telling me stories about how their partners and loved ones were supposed to be doing what they wanted them to do. 'This' was showing me just how deep within the dream of separateness the human mind buries itself. It was also showing me that there is no problem outside of thought. There is only a vibrantly alive mystery called life, which is constantly moving within an immovable peace and quietness.

One insight after another was being revealed during this time, yet I saw that there was nothing to hold onto, and no "me" to hold onto any of it. There was, and still is, the sense that nothing is Scott's, and that this is not Scott's life. There is only 'This,' appearing as everything.

During these months, I would wake up each morning with no conscious intention to write a book or anything at all with regard to spirituality. Yet before I knew what was happening, my fingers were typing. Words were spilling out onto the page. During this time, I met a friend whom I lovingly call "my real teacher," Tom. He did not teach me anything. He and I engaged in an incredible frenzy of inquiry in an online chat room, on the phone, and in emails. I watched all my illusions die, one dream after another, including the illusion of being a spiritual teacher or being someone who is "awakened" or "present." I saw that thought does not accept anything, only presence does. I realized that once the truth takes hold, it is relentless. It wants to reveal everything that is false. Yet I saw that only another thought would care about any of that. I came to realize a deep quietness as my true nature. Every aspect of the dream died until there was only 'This'—this loving quietness which was, and is, still expressing itself. It is as if that quietness wrote this book. This quietness knows that the entire story told above is only a dream of thought. It is not who I am.

Even the Oneness experience is not non-duality. It isn't true Oneness. It is just an experience. So I beg you, the reader, to see it that way. See all experiences for what they are, passing, temporary phenomena. Each experience has a beginning and an end. But the truth to which this book points is more like the space within and through which all temporary thoughts, emotions, states, and experiences come and go. Freedom is not an experience.

About this Book

A new truth is not being presented in this book. No truth is being presented. The truth cannot be presented, it can only be pointed to, and it is everywhere, as who we are and everything around us. By "truth," I don't mean an idea. Ideas come and go within what you are. What you are can never be named. If you name it, you become another idea. When you are free of all fixed mental positions about who you are, who others are, and what life is, you are free. You are free to celebrate and include all ideas, while being attached to none of them. As all lines of division (mental and otherwise) are seen through, all that is left is love. This is love's quiet revolution. Love is our real nature.

This book is pointing to the truth in the same way other non-duality or enlightenment books point to it. Nobody can claim this truth because nobody is here. If this book does nothing more than help you inquire, or point you in the direction of other teachers or teachings that help you inquiry and realize that who you are is inseparable from this present moment and from the rest of life, then it has fulfilled its purpose, surely.

Some will find this book meaningless. Others may be offended by it because it does not reflect back to them the mental story of their particular religion, tradition, practice, or method. In some places, it may challenge the very truth of those things. Still others will see that this book points directly to the truth. Whether it is seen as meaningless, offensive, or enlightening does not matter. "Meaningless," "offensive," and "enlightening" come only from some point of reference within the dream. Ultimately, this book points to the jumping off of all points of reference into the liberation of what is really true.

I state in the book that the spiritual search is self-centered. The word self-centeredness, as it is used in this book, is not a moral judgment. It is a description of how thought is often self-involved. The notion that the search is self-centered is not meant as an insult to you if you see yourself as a spiritual seeker. The dream of "Scott" spent quite some time seeking. Every human seeks in one way or another. Some spiritual searching may be necessary in order to realize that it is not necessary. If you are searching, allow your desire for the truth to burn up every false idea standing in the way of the realization that enlightenment is right now. When I state that the search is self-centered, I am merely pointing you to a reality which must be faced at some point along the journey. True enlightenment is the realization of no self. Thus, there is no self to search for or find the truth. There is only the truth, which is realized when the dream of a separate self dissolves and there is a realization that all there is, is this utterly simple and extraordinary life, happening now. To believe otherwise is to feed into the dream of self that lives in time and that falsely places itself at the center of life.

This book is not intended as authority of any kind. The fact that I sometimes use the word "you" may sound as if authority is speaking. No, "you" is merely used as a choice of pronouns. Because these chapters were written separately, with no intention of making them into a book at the time they were written, you will find various pronouns used throughout the book. In certain chapters, I may address the reader as "you," "ego" or "spiritual seeker." In others, I may use the word "I" when inquiring within. In others, I may use "we." From where this body and mind sits, there is no "you," "we," or "me." There is only 'This.' The real truth is that, no matter what pronoun is being used, this book is speaking to the deeper truth of who you are. It is speaking to your essence, beyond any thoughts that separate life into illusory parts such as author and reader, spiritual teacher and seeker, or me and you.

Do not expect this book to make logical sense either. It may or may not. If you are looking for a spiritual book that tells a linear story or makes sense to the analytical mind, look elsewhere. You may find contradictions in this book. Instead of seeking ways to clarify those contradictions, notice the space in which those contradictions arise. This book points to that space. That space is your very beingness. It is who you are beyond your thoughts or the words in this book. It is 'This.' If the word 'This' bothers or confuses you, you may have found the right book. The human mind is identified with thought. It is constantly looking for objects, thoughts, and words that it already knows. Thought makes an identity out of what it knows, and then looks for the world to confirm its identity. It creates an illusory separate self through this identification process. This illusion called ego is therefore nothing more than a set of thoughts which keeps alive a dream that there is a person at the center of life, separate from everything else. In truth, it is all One and there is no separate self. Suffering arises directly from this dream of separation. If you do not yet see that to which the word 'This' is pointing, simply continue reading.

You will find that certain concepts and phrases are repeated often in the book. This is not by mistake. This book is not presenting new ideas or information. It is speaking directly to beingness. Thus, it is pointing to the relaxation of your busy mind so that the peace that is your natural state can be realized. The mind, however, may resist or argue with all or part of what is said in the book. Repeating certain concepts and phrases helps the mind relax and realize that its arguments come from unwillingness to rest into the natural state of peace to which the book is pointing. No positions are taken in this book. This book is not trying to convince you of anything. It is merely asking you to notice what already is.

If this book serves its purpose, it will totally disarm your intellect so that love can be fully realized and suffering can be seen for the illusion that it is. Read this book with your whole being. Read slowly, letting the words point you to the feeling of beingness and aliveness in your body and mind. After reading a paragraph, stop and sit with the words or go about the business of life. Let your heart read these words and let the words bypass the constantly moving mind that you have been using to make sense out of life. Have you noticed that you have not figured life out yet? Good. You can't. This book points to the end of the whole search to figure it out, and to the radiant mystery in which searching, finding, and everything else arise and fall.

At its most basic level, this book is an inquiry. Rather than outward authority, it was written inwardly, as a demolition project, destroying every illusion standing in the way of enlightenment. The book points to the fact that there is nothing to hold onto despite the insights that arise on the so-called spiritual path. It is simply asking into the emptiness the questions, "Who am I?" "What is God?" "Is anything separate?" and "Does any of that matter?" Far from answering those questions, this book points to the space in which those questions arise and fall. The truth lies there.

Are you ready to inquire? If you are, please continue reading. But if you are thoroughly enjoying the dream of self, close this book instead and continue enjoying the dream.

You are not a thought, feeling, experience, reaction, identity, role, ego, or process. You are the radiant mystery within which those things arise. This mystery has been obscured by a self-centered story and the illusion of separateness. I invite you to wake up to this moment, allow this dream self to dissolve, and discover the Oneness, the unconditioned love that is who you truly are.

— Scott Kiloby

The Insanity of Becoming

*I have lived on the lip of insanity, wanting to know
reasons, knocking on a door. It opens. I've been
knocking from the inside.*

— Rumi

*If a spiritual practice is not designed to awaken you
to this moment where life is, then it is an escape from,
and therefore a denial of, life.*

— Scott Kiloby

One
WHAT HAVE YOU BEEN SEEKING?

You are what observes, not what you observe.

— *Buddha*

What we are looking for . . . is what is looking.
— *St. Francis of Assisi*

In this moment, you realize what does not need to be practiced to exist. This is the easiest, simplest, and most obvious truth. What has kept it a secret throughout the ages is its absolute simplicity and its immediate availability.

— *Gangaji*

What have you been looking for all your life? Have you wanted peace, contentment, happiness, love, and joy? How much have you given of your money, your time, and your energy to find these things? How many books have you read, how many arguments, debates, meditation sittings, church services, meetings, vacations, retreats, relationships, sexual encounters, jobs, promotions, drugs, foods, diets, material items, thoughts, dreams, and goals were pursued or indulged in with the hope that, from these things, you would receive what you were seeking? Have you been looking for yourself—for the "better," "happier," or "more spiritual" you?

Have you realized that "better," "happier," and "more spiritual" are only presently arising ideas? They have no objective reality, except within your own mind-made, time-based dream of self. The ego is a set of thoughts. It is a dream of time, which means a dream of mind. I also call the ego "the dream self." There is no such thing as an ego or dream self. Yet the words ego and dream self are used to describe this set of thoughts that is looking for a more complete version of itself. You, the ego, will never find completion on the level of time because time is merely mind. Thought. You are not real as a person separate from the rest of life. "You" are a thought that is chasing another thought called "better," "happier," or "more spiritual."

By its very nature, the ego is unfulfilled and unfulfillable. You will never reach the ultimate version of yourself. Thought will not let you. That would mean the end of the ego—the end of you. Even if you reach some goal you have placed on yourself, the content of what you are seeking will simply change, creating another carrot out there beyond your reach. This is what the ego is, and what it does. It is a carrot making machine. It is a set of thoughts from which you derive a sense of self which always feels incomplete. These presently arising thoughts keep the search for a more complete self alive, which keeps the ego making more and different carrots. Today, the carrot may be a slimmer waist, tomorrow it may be a new husband, and next year it may be enlightenment. Carrots, that is all.

The Rat on the Wheel

The ego is like a rat on a wheel. The rat totally believes he is going somewhere, yet he is only spinning around and around. He does not realize that there is such a thing as "off the wheel." He only sees the wheel. He only sees his own dream of becoming. Similarly, in its mind-made dream of future fulfillment, the ego's search for fulfillment in time is only a mental dream. You are simply looking for fulfillment within your own thoughts. You never get there. You cannot. The wheel of self will not let you. The wheel is the time-based mind, and its only goal is to keep spinning, to keep becoming. This illusory, separate dream self is built from—and fueled by—a thought-made sense of lack, which feeds into mental projection towards future, which in turn feeds the sense of lack because you never quite "get there," which in turn feeds the projection towards future. You are only ever chasing your own thoughts, which you mistake for reality.

This constant chasing after one's own thoughts is insanity. There is nothing inherently unhealthy with goals if the present moment remains primary. But if you are searching for a sense of self in these presently arising ideas about future, you have reduced this radiant mystery called you to a thought or set of thoughts. You are indulging in a self-centered dream that perpetuates lack. This lack will continue fueling the illusory search for self in thoughts until it is seen clearly for what it is—a dream of self-centeredness.

Do you see the madness of this search? Do you see your attachment to outcomes? Do you realize that you cannot find yourself in time? The only thing you could ever find is a rearrangement of the thoughts in your head. When it appears to your mind that you have found sadness, you are simply experiencing identification with an arrangement of sad thoughts. When it appears to your mind that you have found happiness, you are experiencing attachment to happy thoughts. Thought is story. On its face, this makes sense, doesn't it? You are not an idea, or set of ideas. Isn't it time to realize this deeply? Isn't it time to see if there is true happiness and fulfillment beyond this dream of becoming—beyond this dream of self? There is!

You Are What You Have Been Seeking

For every moment you spend thinking about yourself, and thought is virtually always about the self, you are missing this moment—the eternal present—and the beautiful manifestations of life within it. You are missing who you truly are. You cannot find true peace, love, and joy in the future. It does not exist in time. You are peace. You are love. You are joy. Now. How do you find or lose that which you are? The notions of finding and losing are thoughts that arise within who you truly are. If there is something in you right now saying, "But I don't feel that peace, love, and joy," that is because the search for peace, love, and joy is obscuring the peace, love, and joy that is who you truly are. Maddening, isn't it? It is maddening until it is seen clearly, at which point it becomes undeniably true.

How can you find yourself in time? "Future" is simply a presently arising thought. It is a dream conjured up by the ego to keep the illusory search for self going. Every thought or search that attempts to move away from this moment, where life is, obscures the very life that you are now. But even that is not true. You cannot escape or move away from this moment. It is impossible. Thought has trapped you within its virtual reality. You are the rat. You falsely believe you are going somewhere. You do not see that there is such a thing as "off the wheel." The truth is, you are already whole and complete. "Off the wheel" is your true nature in this moment, but the mental movement of becoming has been obscuring this reality. Figuratively speaking, life is playing a joke on you. It is not funny as long as suffering results from it. But when you are off the wheel, it is absolutely hilarious.

You are an extraordinary and ordinary mystery, abiding in peace, love, and joy in this moment. That which you have been looking for is already within you. Every attempt at looking to thoughts of past to define you is a misperception of who you really are in this moment. Every thought that the future will fulfill you is deceiving you. As Jesus said, "the kingdom of God is within you."[1] The fullness of life is already here. You are it.

This truth is not just another thought or belief. When you close this book, if you simply think the thought, "This moment is who I am," that may help point you to this moment. But ultimately, if you keep what is said here on the level of thought only, you will just be adding another thought onto the pile of past thoughts already known as "you." You will miss the simple truth completely. Then you may insist to yourself and to others that you are present. But presence does not make such claims about itself, only self-centered thought does. Ultimately, I am pointing to that which sees all thought including the thought "I am present." I am pointing to the awareness that you are—the ground of beingness prior to all thought. It is that which is looking from your eyes right now. Can you sense that beingness? Don't think about it, just sense it. Realize you are it. The truth is intimately close and immediately available as the essence of life within you right now. Any attempt to go looking for it in thought obscures it.

This book is not a prescription to do anything, including become more present. There is no such thing as becoming present. Becoming implies future and effort. This book is an invitation to notice what is already here. There is no effort or future involved in noticing what is already happening now. I am simply asking whether you notice the light of awareness within you that is already on. It has always been on. You have always been here in this moment. Thought has just been telling a story of self in time. Just notice what is already arising now, including any inattentiveness to what is arising.

Thought is not the problem. Suffering happens when you believe thoughts that tell you that something should be happening other than what is happening. That includes the thought that tells you that you should be more present than you are now, that you should be more spiritual, enlightened, or closer to God. To ever believe that something should be other than the way it is right now is insanity. How can something be other than the way it is? That is impossible. You cannot get any closer to God than you are right now. God is timeless. The phrase, "The presence of God," is pointing to the fact that God is only ever right here, right now, in this moment. Your dream of becoming is not about God, spirituality, or enlightenment. It is ego.

If a thought arises that tells you that something needs to happen other than what is happening, recognize it for what it is: a presently arising thought. Start telling the truth. Only the truth will set you free. Reality is right now. Time is merely mind. This truth, once it is realized deeply within, knocks you off your feet and out of your mind-made story of becoming. You then realize that there never was a spiritual path. I do not have a path. You do not have a path. This is not my life. That is not your life. There is only One Life. 'This.' Now. Here. One. God. You made the idea of a path up along the way to keep the focus on you. You have been like a dog chasing his own tail—like the rat on the wheel. Your mind was doing all this so that you would not realize that the peace that you were seeking is already who you are underneath that seeking energy. When I say "who you are," those too are just words. The simple truth is that there is no separate you outside of thought. You arise as a separate person only when you think yourself into existence. A quiet mind reveals that there is only 'This.' Thought will never understand that. Only you (awareness) will. This awareness knows that what is being said here is pointing directly to what is true. Thought might disagree, but you know. All your life you thought you were your thoughts. But they are not who you are and they cannot tell you who you are. They arise within who you are.

Thought is not your enemy. Do not try to stop or suppress thought. It will not work. Just watch what arises. That which is aware of thought is who you are. Through this awakening, you realize in a way that can never be fully explained that you are much less than you think you are, and yet much more than your mind could ever have imagined in its dream.

From that watching within, a heart knowing takes over that is far deeper and more loving than the mind's seeking energy and its false sense of certainty. You can then allow thought to express that knowing, while understanding fully that the words, concepts, names, and descriptions are not it. They merely point to it.

This book is just a story of 'This.' When I use the words 'This,' God, One, enlightenment, self-realization, liberation, or presence throughout this book, realize that these are also just presently arising thoughts. They are stories. As Gangaji has eloquently expressed: There is nothing wrong with stories. They are neither good nor bad. They are just not ultimately true.

The truth is that you are this beingness that *is* in this moment, not the thoughts that arise within it. If you can see the ultimate truth to which these stories are pointing, by all means put this book down. Put all spiritual books down. If not, keep reading until you see for yourself the insanity of becoming.

Two
THE END OF THE SPIRITUAL SEARCH

When the person is no more, when the search is undone, when the demand for life to be anything other than what it is collapses, the noise and silence, the freedom and bondage, the Yin and the Yang are all seen to be illusory, simply the mind's attempt to cut the world up into manageable little pieces, and the truth is revealed: there is only the whole.

— *Jeff Foster*

The spiritual search is a product of the moving mind. When I say "spiritual search," I don't just mean those people who are actively engaged in seeking enlightenment or even a closer relationship with God. I mean all humans, everywhere. Everyone is seeking something, as Chapter One pointed out. If you believe that something is missing in your life now and that the future holds the key to your contentment (whether through a job, relationship, material success, or anything else), you are on a spiritual search, as that term is defined in this book. This search is based in separation—in the idea that you are a person, separate from the rest of life, who must reach some goal in time in order to be complete, whole. A truly quiet mind allows you to see that you are not separate from what you seek. You are not separate from the whole. So the notion of seeking something as if you do not already have it is the dream of self. The self is a dream of temporal and spatial separation, created by thought.

The Dream of Spatial Separation

What does it mean to say that there is no separation spatially? It means that there are no separate things situated in space, even though separation appears. Only thought makes it appear that there are separate things. When a thought arises, the separate thing arises.

This is not a belief you come upon through persuasion by some teacher or fancy words in a book. It is an actual realization. You see it clearly when the mind stops. Actually, "you" do not see it in the way a person sees another object because, when separation is seen through, every separate thing is seen through, especially the notion of "you" as a separate self. It is seen. That is all that can be said. In fact, the mind doesn't even have to stop in order to see this. Take one moment and notice that no matter what object you see, you only know it as a separate object because a thought is presently arising.

The "you" I'm referring to is awareness, not "you" the person or story. What is awareness? Drop all thought for one moment. What is looking is awareness. Now, notice thought *as it is arising*. Notice that it tells you that there is a separate object. Notice that when the thought falls away, you cannot know that there is a separate object anymore. Separation is thought. Thought is separation.

You are not a separate thing at the center of life, despite what your thoughts tell you. In the awakening into Oneness, you see that life is living you, and it has no center. Spatial separation is a creation of thought. Any suffering experienced in your relationships with the illusory separate "others" in your life is a creation of self-centered thought. All suffering ends in the realization that there is no separate "you" to suffer.

The Dream of Temporal Separation

What does it mean to say there is no separation temporally? It means that there is no such thing as the past or future except through presently arising thoughts. As expressed by Augustine of Hippo, known as a church father in Christianity, God exists outside of time in the eternal present. Life is only ever now. So any attempt by the mind to move into past or future to find God, or self, or truth is the dream. This illusion is occurring simply because the mind is moving. No other reason. It is like a movie playing in your head, where you create and maintain the story of a separate self by replaying parts of the reel that have already played (the past). You attempt to control the characters and the storyline by speeding up the reel to the parts that have not yet played (the future). This movie is a dream of self-centeredness.

The spiritual search does not end because you find God, or self, or truth at some later point in the movie. It ends when the reel stops, and you see life the way that it really is now. The truth is you do not have control of life. Control is part of the movie.

The illusion of temporal separation occurs when the mind reaches into past or future. Time is mind. So thought leaves the reality of now in search of some dream of self in past or future. Actually, thought doesn't leave the reality of now at all. Thoughts arise within the present space of now. But this isn't seen, so you really think you are living in time. Thoughts paint the picture that you are visiting the past or future. They give the false impression that the past or future has something to do with your identity. But you never are really visiting the past or future. You are only thinking. These pictures are illusions. If you reach into thought for a sense of self, you are reducing yourself to a set of mental images, memories, pictures . . . illusions.

Is there such a thing as the past or future, as a past "you" or a future "you?" Look at what is happening when you think there is. That's just it. You THINK there is! A thought is arising. The past or future that you claim exists is merely thought. Thought gives the false impression that there are discrete points in time, like past, present, and future. But each of these is a thought. Everything you think about your life is a thought. And all these thoughts happen within an awareness that sees them. This book is pointing to that awareness. Isn't that what you really are? Each time you think of yourself, you are entertaining a mental image. That image, because it arises in dualistic thought, makes you feel separate from life. Regardless of the content, every thought about yourself makes it appear that "you" are in that thought, that you ARE that thought. In order to think about yourself this way, you have to suppress the rest of life. You have to suppress all other thoughts. So each thought of yourself is a thought of a separate person existing totally independently of life itself. And that is impossible. You are life.

The separation, because it is based in illusion, causes suffering. This is why peoples' lives are so often full of conflict, struggle, and searching. Thought is comparing the past (the dream) to what is now (reality). Conflict arises immediately between what was and what truly is. Thought is also playing fearful future scenarios and following mind-made ideals of future, all of which are in direct conflict with what is in this moment. Most people live exclusively within the moving mind, missing the eternal present completely. Conflict arises whenever there is separation. Oneness is the truth. Anything which opposes the truth causes suffering.

So temporal separation is essentially not realizing who you are in this moment. It is an identity crisis. This is why the realization of Oneness, in the moment of enlightenment, is accompanied by the loss of the dream of a separate self. In one instant, everything becomes clear. It is all One. Suffering in time (e.g., "My past haunts me" or "I fear the future") is a creation of thought. So in awakening, the whole notion that who you are has anything to do with the past or the future, which are only presently arising thoughts, is seen as a dream. Seeing through temporal separation sounds like a fancy realization. It just means no longer believing your thoughts about a self living in time. When a thought about the story of you in past or future arises, see it for what it is: just a thought (providing a false sense of separation). The thought only seems true or real when you believe it, follow it, and engage it. Many people believe that they won't be able to function if they stop believing thoughts about their personal story or they won't be able to remember anything. This is a false myth. You will still call yourself "Sally" and you will still be able to tell your story. But you won't identify with that story. Your memory remains. It is identification with memory that is seen through.

In awakening out of the belief in temporal separation, seeking towards the future falls away. When the word "awakening" is used in this book, it is not referring to a mystical event that happens only to special people with special enlightened stories. *See Chapter 23: You the Unnamable Opening.* Awakening is not a mystical term at all. To be awake just means to see. So when a thought arises, see it for what it is—just a thought. Do not treat Oneness as some big experience you have to find in your future. Oneness is not about a person who finds something special within his story. Be clear: when the thought arises that you need to keep seeking into the future in order to have a Oneness experience, see that for what it is: a thought arising in the space of now. You are like the space in which thoughts about Oneness and awakening happen. It's that simple.

Belief Keeps the Search Alive

Oneness is not true because you want it to be true. It is not true because it feels good. It is not a new belief. All of that is part of the dream. It is true because it just is. The One is beyond belief. The truth has nothing to do with whether you like it or do not like it. Whether you like it or not is your dream.

Belief will actually keep you from seeing this truth. Belief exists within the mind-made self. It separates you from me; you from your annoying co-worker; the Christian from the Buddhist; the Catholic from the Baptist; the capitalist from the socialist; the black from the white; and the gay from the straight. Do not get upset with me for telling you this. You already know this deep within. You have just been telling a story that denies it. Your belief system, and your agreement and disagreement, are just food for your own ego. They simply keep alive the illusory self-centered search. Find out whether this is true. Look within your own mind. Look, don't think. Whether it is true or not does not matter in the end. This is your dream. If you find it to be not true, you can simply brush me off as some loony guy who is "way out there." Then you can get back to your belief system, and the separation it engenders.

The truth does not need a defense, right? Ultimately, I am not here to persuade you of anything. Only belief needs a defense. All beliefs need a defense within the egoic mind. As with all forms, beliefs are shaky because they are based in something less than absolute truth. So the energy of defense is needed to strengthen them. This fuels the search, because you are on a track to prove that your already-established belief system is true. You are on a track to prove self. I am not trying to convince you that you should not believe anything. That would just be another belief. I am pointing you to the truth beyond what you believe or do not believe about the truth. This is the truth of who you are. Beliefs arise and dissolve within 'This.' You are that which is reading this book, not the beliefs or thoughts you have about it. Do you see the distinction? Do not conclude that you see it. Conclusion is just another word for belief. Look deeply at the beingness which these words are pointing to. That beingness is who you really are. It knows no separation.

The Dream Dies and Truth Is Realized

What does all this have to do with the spiritual search? In order to find what is true, you must be willing to look within yourself, to see the whole movement of self operating, and separating itself in space and time. The search is born from this separation.

In each moment, look at your discontent, your constant becoming, your dissatisfaction, your conflict, your obsessive preoccupation with past and future, and your resistance to now. The self is a mind-made construct, which believes thoughts about how you are somehow separate from the life that you see around you. This separateness, because it is a dream, creates the illusory sense of not enough. This sense of lack sends you searching in time, which means in mind. You will never find fulfillment on the level of time because you are searching only within a dream of thought. The main goal of this dream is to keep its end from happening. "You" are just one of the ideas within that dream. The idea of "you" is searching for the idea of "fulfillment." This whole system is designed to continue the insanity of becoming because an illusion cannot find another illusion. True fulfillment is not an idea. It cannot be found through ideas. It is beyond ideas. It is that which sees the idea of "you" and the idea of "fulfillment."

Being aware of that whole movement of self allows you to see it for what it truly is—a movement of ideas. It is mind movement, nothing else. You see that the ambition of becoming, whether it is based in capitalism or spirituality, is self-centered.

If, in one instant, you saw clearly that you are not separate from all that is, would you continue searching? Would there be any judging, comparing, discontent, conflict, struggle, war? Would you be reading this spiritual book? What if all your attempts at searching for a better, more complete self in future are actually obscuring the truth of who you really are in this moment? Isn't that worth looking at? Again, I am not asking you to believe anything. Please do not believe a word I say. I am asking, don't you want to look: I mean really, really look at what is here, what is happening and not happening? What is absolutely true?

If so, be a fool for the truth. Be willing to look at everything, starting with your own illusions, your own mind movements, and the way that you avoid emotions instead of facing them directly. Looking means seeing the mind movements in the moment they happen. It means staring directly into the emotional wounds that you have been trying to escape through relationships, sex, jobs, beliefs, methods, food, drugs and the like. When I say stare directly into these emotional wounds, I do not mean that you should revisit the past. You can, but you must see that the past is only a presently arising thought. That is what is true. Simply watch these wounds as they manifest in response to some trigger in this moment.

Ask yourself whether each thought is absolutely true. Is it absolutely true that life and circumstances should be the way you want them to be? That is the dream, isn't it? Is your mind actually covering up the reality of what is with some self-centered interpretation? If it is not doing this, then you have nothing to lose by looking at your mind. But if you really want to know the truth, you will look in each moment at what your mind is doing. You will notice that what you consider to be reality is whatever story you believe in this moment. You will look at each emotion as it is arising, and face it directly and fully. You will notice the mental stories you are telling about emotions. You will notice when you are trying to justify, rationalize, or think away bad thoughts and emotions. The mind is always trying to escape, and in its escape, it welcomes more suffering because reality is not faced directly. You are running from the truth.

You will see that this whole movement of self is a spiritual search. That set of thoughts in your head could be summed up with two words: "not enough." The search is fueled by those thoughts. You are creating the problem with thought, and then looking for the solution with thought. As Albert Einstein said, "You can't solve a problem with the same mind that created it." As a friend of mine put it once, "Believing that you can find yourself through thought is like standing on a board and trying to pick yourself up by picking the board up." Futile.

Enlightenment is not about reaching the satisfactory conclusion of the story you have created in your own head. It is not about your projection or search. It is not about discovering that your belief system is right. In that case, you would only be convincing yourself that your own thoughts are true. Enlightenment is not about the journey, path, or the destination. It is realized when you step off the path suddenly and completely into the truth of who you really are in this moment. It is realizing that it is all One, happening now, and the One includes all the spiritual experiences, all the highs and lows of life, all the ups and downs, all the thoughts and emotions. It includes everything.

Seeking arises when you start searching for an aspect of the One, mistakenly believing that you lack something. It arises when you get stuck or become fixated with any particular fragment of the whole. To be fixated on a fragment of the whole means to be stuck in a state, looking for the end of the state or for some other state. If anger is arising, you go looking for the end of anger or for peace. If sadness arises, you go looking for the end of sadness or for happiness. If you experience happiness or a spiritual high, you go searching to recreate it again. If you receive praise or acknowledgment in a role or job, you seek more praise and acknowledgment. You feel diminished when you do not find it. Suffering arises the moment you attempt to escape what is. Enlightenment simply means no more escaping. It means allowing the awareness within you to face directly and no longer resist in any way whatever mental and emotional suffering is arising now.

Whenever you become fixated on finding, having, or maintaining an experience, high, plateau, state, status, role, image, understanding, or a particular belief or set of thoughts about yourself or life, you are stuck. You are fighting the universal law of impermanence. Life is changing and moving constantly. When you are stuck, you are fixating on an aspect of the One. You are trying to stop or capture some aspect of this moving and changing life, rather than simply being open to whatever is arising now. This causes suffering because the idea that you can capture anything is an illusion. Suffering perpetuates the spiritual search as you go looking in thought for the end of suffering. You continue being the rat on the wheel, giving yourself more time, and more becoming, which is more self. This is why the spiritual search is self-centered. It is all about you, and how you do not have what you want, and do not want what you have.

Do not try to end the search. Only thought would attempt that. Simply notice every thought which arises that tells you that something needs to happen in the future for you to be free. These are lies. Notice the awareness which is looking at these lies. That awareness is the truth.

The realization to which the word "enlightenment" is pointing is lived when you face directly whatever is arising. It is lived when you realize that you are the opening in which every experience, high, plateau, state, status, role, image, understanding, thought, belief, feeling and everything else happens.

Noticing this constant movement away from this moment allows you to see that the self is a dream of time, and therefore of mind. When the movement of the mind is seen in each moment, this fixation on thought, and therefore on self, drops away by its own volition. The illusion of separateness dies. The whole takes over. God takes over. Not as some fantastic new belief system. Not a fairytale. No, not at all. The truth takes over, with more love, peace, joy, and inclusiveness than you could have ever imagined. This truth is not about you as a separate entity. You are not at the center of life. And yet, paradoxically, the truth of life cannot be realized without you. It is realized through you, and as you, as One Life. This truth is seen only when you and your preoccupation with self are out of the way. It is the realization that you are not separate from the whole.

In one fell swoop, you see that the whole spiritual search was an attempt to keep the self-centeredness alive. Through the search, you kept the focus on you, including where you came from, where you are going, what you know, how close you are to God, whether you are better today than yesterday, and whether you will be better tomorrow than you are today. As long as you were thinking these thoughts, you were keeping "you" at the center of life within your dream.

Do you see your thoughts about who you are yet? Notice the dream. Don't engage it with analysis. That would just be more dreaming. Just watch. And then notice what is looking. What is looking is who you really are. It is love itself. This love swallows everything which is not true. So it devours you and your spiritual search. If there is only THAT, and YOU ARE THAT, what is there left to search for? The spiritual search ends through this realization that there is no separate you, and there is not, and never was, a search. You made that up. It was simply thought. Nothing wrong with thought, but the truth is the truth.

The spiritual search does not end because you read this or some other book about how it is supposed to end, or because you understand conceptually that it is a self-centered dream. It ends because it is realized deeply that the search is and always was a dream. This realization is beyond thought. It can happen in one moment or gradually. But when it happens, you are done. It is over. Gone. Bye-bye.

And, of course, that is where the real fun begins. The search is the self. The self obscures the truth, which means it obscures love. So love is what is left when the search ends.

Three
THE EGO'S MESSIANIC PROJECTIONS

The projections of others do not belong to me. I am never a teacher, just a lover who has been given a glimpse of the Beloved.

— Llewellyn Vaughan-Lee

Spiritual seekers tend to make spiritual teachers into messiahs. A seeker may compare this teacher to that teacher, falsely believing that this teacher has something to give him and that one does not. He may believe that a teacher is larger than life or that the teacher is or has authority. This seeker has not yet realized that the truth is already within him, and that the only thing even the best teacher can do is point to that which is already within.

The best spiritual teachers know that they are not truly teachers, and will constantly undermine any authority which is placed upon them. If the seeker does not see this, he may set a course for what can only be called worship or ego projection. Thus, he becomes fixated on Eckhart Tolle, Buddha or some other teacher not realizing that those are merely vessels through which the truth is expressing itself. In order to be free from this trap, he must see the self-centeredness built into these egoic projections. These projections are obscuring the truth within. These vessels called "teachers" are merely pointing the seeker to an exquisite truth which is immediately accessible as the very life within him. Missing this means missing everything.

Only seeking energy would make a teacher into a messianic figure. The word "seeker" is not being used here in a derogatory sense. Every human seeks to one degree or another. Some seeking may be necessary for the liberation from self to be realized. The term "seeker" simply means the movement of the energy of seeking within a body and mind. A seeker often seeks something outside himself on which to focus. This focus is a denial of the love within him. A messiah is essentially a projection of an ego that is still seeking, which perceives a sense of lack within. The seeker then projects onto the teacher all sorts of attributes which the seeker seeks for himself: enlightenment, truth, peace, love, freedom, or joy. As long as he is focused on some concept that he perceives to be outside of him, and that he is trying to attain, including a book, a teacher, or scripture, no inward looking can take place. The seeker does not see that he is feeding his own sense of lack with these outward projections.

The seeker essentially projects all of his love on his teacher so that he does not have to face the full weight of the love that is already within him, but which is being obscured by this energy of projecting. Projecting is seeking. The seeker may attempt to derive a sense of self based on the teacher or method he follows, and how long he has been following the teacher or method. He may compare himself to his teacher, and to other seekers whom he perceives to have false teachers, preachers, methods, or gods. He may find himself challenging others, including other seekers, teachers, and religions, all in an attempt to feed a sense of lack within. All of this is coming from an insecure self-image—an image that is entirely false, but remains unseen as long as the seeker is projecting and seeking something outside of himself. He has not realized the wholeness of life that is already within him, so he keeps separation alive by projecting, comparing, challenging, arguing and debating. To the ego, all this movement appears to be bringing him closer to the truth. In reality, it is moving him away from the realization that he is the truth. In such cases, the seeker will often vehemently deny he is doing any of this. After all, ego is unconscious mind movement and it must deny the truth in order to keep the false alive.

Are you a seeker? Are you projecting the love that you are onto your teacher? Notice any thoughts of comparison in you, between yourself and other people, seekers, or teachers. Notice how you come to defend certain teachers and argue that other teachers, methods, practices and religions are false. What are you defending, a sense of self? Investigate this person within you who is doing all this defending. Realize there is no one there, except a set of thoughts, emotions, and sensations, each appearing one after the other. In realizing that, you realize there is also no one there in the teacher or the other seeker. In this realization, you realize there is nothing to defend. There is only One Life. The divisions and separations are completely within your own thoughts. They are not "out there" in the teachers, teachings, and religions. In this seeing true love and compassion replace the projecting, comparing, challenging, arguing, debating, and seeking.

When the truth is realized in you, you will see that there really is no such thing as a teacher, seeker, student, or messiah. Remember, "truth" in this book is not a mental conclusion. It is freedom from all fixed mental conclusions. Teacher, seeker, student, and messiah are all outward egoic projections (and even the ego is a projection, an inward one, so to speak). They are conclusions. These projections are literally created by a mind that lives in separation, a mind that believes it lacks something in comparison to someone else. No teacher can give you what you already are. Teachings, as mere pointers, are poor substitutes for inward inquiry. Once inquiry (which is discussed in a later chapter) takes hold, you will no longer need any teacher or teachings. You certainly will not need this book. It was written as a simple pointer which says, "Do you see that you are the truth and that you lack nothing?"

Four
THE SPIRITUAL SEEKER IS A NEGOTIATOR

What a blessing to have realized that the flowering of human consciousness happens only in my absence.
— Scott Kiloby

My teachings are easy to understand and easy to put into practice. Yet your intellect will never grasp them, and if you try to practice them, you'll fail.
— Lao-tzu, Tao Te Ching[2]

The spiritual seeker is a negotiator. He negotiates with life itself. He does not realize that there is only One Life and that he is that. He is the very life he is seeking. The negotiation takes place because he sees himself as separate from that which he seeks. His mind divides life into illusory fragments, then he sets out to find what he believes he lacks. He does not realize that he created the lack through thought. He bargains with life or God, and with so-called "spiritual principles," in order to get something in return for his spiritual investment called "the search." He is looking to make himself whole. He is seeking fulfillment not realizing that fulfillment is his natural state underneath all the energy of seeking.

He creates the separateness through thought. He thinks his freedom, joy, peace, compassion, acceptance, humility and love are somehow "out there" in life, in future, not realizing that these are simply words expressing his natural state in this moment. He creates the problem with thought (i.e., the idea that he is separate from the whole) and then sets out to solve it with thought (i.e., the idea that the future will bring completion). This is the insanity of becoming.

To go searching for ourselves in spirituality is a natural course for humanity to take. This seeking energy is derived from a natural, evolutionary movement within us to realize freedom—to realize who we really are. The ego hijacks this search, however, and leaves the mind spinning in its own virtual reality of becoming. This keeps self-centeredness in place and obscures the truth. Man must mature spiritually at some point and realize ultimately that he is that which he seeks. He is already free. What he finds in this realization called "enlightenment" is not a better, more improved version of his ego in the future. To even search for that is ego-centered. He finds reality—the timeless present moment. He realizes that he is not at all separate from life and that there is nothing to seek. He realizes Oneness, God, or whatever one wishes to call it. It is beyond any name or thought we place on it.

When thought stops negotiating with life and with surrender, acceptance, peace, love, joy, compassion, humility and freedom, the seeker realizes that he already has those things because those are attributes of his natural state in this moment. This natural state is realized only when all searching and seeking stop completely–when this moment is seen in all its fullness. "How shall I grasp it?" was asked by a student to Zen master Panchadasi, to which he replied: "Do not grasp it. That which remains when there is no more grasping is who you truly are."

When this truth is realized, the seeker does not become perfect. The whole notion of seeking to be perfect is an illusion created by the ego. This keeps the search alive because the ego knows it can never attain perfection. This non-attainment gives the ego more time, which is perfectly designed to keep the spiritual search going and therefore to keep self-centeredness in place. Giving the ego more time means giving it more mind. More mind means more story, resistance, searching, dissatisfaction, and lack. The ego will never know the fullness of life because it is in the business of denying life—denying the reality of this moment. It is cut off from life energy, stuck in the thought realms of past, future, and resistance to now. Enlightenment is the waking up to reality now, and therefore it is beyond belief, including the belief in a separate self that is becoming better or waking up over time. As Philip K. Dick once said, "Reality is that which, when you stop believing in it, doesn't go away." Thus, in waking up to reality, there is no dream self left to chase after the dream called perfection.

Surrender

During the spiritual search the ego becomes very sophisticated. The whole goal of the ego is to get something in return from all of its endeavors. This includes the spiritual search. It wants something from its investment in spirituality—more specifically its belief that the future will bring a better, more spiritual self or a closer relationship with God. The search is as self-centered as any endeavor into which the ego sinks its teeth. It is still all about the "me" and what this "me" can gain from its spiritual investment. When the ego becomes spiritually sophisticated, it begins an illusory negotiation with spiritual principles in an attempt to gain something out of it all.

The ego will negotiate with this principle called "surrender," hoping to escape pain or become a more spiritual self. The word "surrender," however, is pointing to an attribute of the natural state, prior to all escaping and seeking energy. It is just another word for presence which is naturally surrendered. "Surrender" is not real as a concept separate from life itself or as anything anyone can apply. Yet the ego makes surrender into something separate from itself so that it can continue searching for it. This keeps the sense of lack in place because the ego is always chasing the carrot known as "surrender."

The ego tries to apply surrender to this or that particular life situation as you would apply a lotion to a rash. It is trying to escape the resistance in which it finds itself. But escape is itself resistance to what is. The ego is resistance. An ego can never reach surrender because true surrender is the absence of ego. It is the absence of resistance. The only way there is ever truly surrender is when there is no longer a separate self trying to attain surrender or escape pain. Pain and resistance must be fully faced in the moment they arise. Anything else is ego.

In its search, the ego knows that it cannot and will not completely surrender. The ego is afraid of total surrender. If there is one thing that scares a person into the illusion of control and resistance, it is the fear that life will go on without her. It will, more easily than ever. Total surrender means the absence of all searching and all applying, which is the absence of ego. There is no one there to search for or apply anything called "surrender." Only an ego would seek or apply something to itself, falsely believing that it is separate from that which it is seeking or applying.

In complete surrender to what is there is only 'This,' the unnamable presence in this moment. There is no you in 'This.' There is only surrender. When the natural state is realized, the concept of surrender becomes null and void. The concept is only important to the spiritual seeker who mistakenly believes that she is separate from surrender and that she must find it.

The whole notion of surrender arises only because the ego is, at its essence, non-surrender. So the ego looks for the opposite of what it is, not realizing that the opposite is merely its own creation. Surrender is no more real than "ego." The ego makes up the concept of surrender to go along with its dream called "the spiritual search." This keeps alive the insanity of becoming "more" surrendered. In true surrender, there is no need for a spiritual search—no need for an illusory movement away from now into some future dream where surrender can be found. There is no need for a concept like surrender.

In true presence, action is taken from the natural state. This is sometimes called "surrendered action." There is no negotiation involved. One does not half surrender or continue obsessing over the problem at hand because that just makes it more complicated. Thought will just keep analyzing, measuring, and attempting to see how it can negotiate a surrender while still maintaining the ego (the thought-based self) in place. Only presence truly surrenders because presence is surrender. Presence drops all thoughts about the situation or it does not. It does not make a problem out of the dropping or not dropping. There is no attachment to the dropping or not dropping. It does not see a problem. It sees only what is arising, and action is taken or it is not. When action is taken, it is taken from natural surrender. Love is what is acting in those moments, not ego.

In true surrender, one does not surrender to be a "better" or "more spiritual" person in return. She does not surrender to please God or get God off her back or to brag to others about how "surrendered" she is. There is no one to negotiate anything in total surrender—no one seeking anything in return for anything. Only egos want something in return. Surrender just surrenders without expectation of gain or reward. In fact, if gain or reward is sought, it is not true surrender.

Surrender is negation of all wanting and needing for anything to be or turn out a certain way. There is nothing to gain and no one to gain anything. To realize the natural state of surrender, there is nothing to do because all doing comes from ego, from resistance itself. To realize enlightenment, there must be a noticing not only of the thoughts that create resistance to what is, but also a noticing of the whole mental strategy of surrendering, which is still ego. There must be a willingness to want nothing from life. And in that nothingness, the fullness of life is gained and the dream self is lost. There is no one there surrendering. There is only surrender, and no one there to make a big deal out of the concept of surrender. All negotiations cease because all separation ceases.

Acceptance

In its spiritual sophistication, the seeker also negotiates with acceptance. He looks for acceptance to give him a more spiritual self, relieve him of pain, or carry him through a rough time. It is still all about personal gain or escape from reality. Acceptance cannot be found in time. The moment you go searching for acceptance in future, you are avoiding this moment. Avoidance of any kind is non-acceptance of what is.

During the search, the seeker may talk about accepting this or accepting that, or how he intends to accept this or is trying to accept that. He thinks a lot about his problems including the problem of not having found acceptance yet. This is clearly self-centeredness. It is all about the "me."

The separate self is essentially a set of mind-made problems including the problem of not having found acceptance yet. Without these mind-made problems, there is no separate self. The ego does not want to live in total acceptance. That would constitute the end of the ego. In full acceptance, there is no separate self (no set of problems). So the ego loves its mind-made problems. And it loves its completely illusory dream that thought will solve those problems. It won't. Thought does not accept. It measures, analyzes, and thinks about the situation of which it is seeking acceptance, but it does not truly accept. Only presence truly accepts. Presence is already acceptance. It does not have to do anything to get to acceptance. Only thought would believe that something needs to be done in order to get to acceptance. This is the dream of time—the insanity of becoming.

Presence drops all thought about the situation or it does not. In any case, no problem is made out of the dropping or not dropping. This may sound like apathy. In truth, is it pure acceptance and therefore unconditional love. Action may still be taken from pure presence in order to influence positive change, but the action comes from energy that is open to what is, not the self-centered energy of resistance, seeking, and excessive analysis.

Resistance causes suffering. This is why the ego sets out on a spiritual journey. But the ego will never find true acceptance once it starts seeking it. Seeking implies effort, time, and escape, which is resistance to what is arising now. The ego is resistance so its seeking energy only fuels ego.

True acceptance happens when there is awareness of not only the thoughts that resist reality (i.e. non-acceptance), but also the entire mental analysis involved in seeking acceptance. This analysis is itself effort and resistance and therefore non-acceptance. Noticing it allows it to fall away on its own. As long as there is a dream self there seeking acceptance, true acceptance cannot be realized. A spiritual seeker who resists what was just said gives himself more years along the spiritual search. He gives himself more time, which is more ego. He is not ready to give up this dream self that believes it is the center of life.

Peace

The seeker may also negotiate with peace in her self-created spiritual journey. She mistakenly believes that peace is something she will attain in the future or through her own actions. In this way, she wants a return on her spiritual investment. The self wants to negotiate with peace so that it can refer to itself as a "peaceful self." There is no such thing. Thought is not truly interested in peace. True peace means the total annihilation of the noisy, thought-based self and its attachment to seeking and judgment. By its very nature, the dream self is non-peace. It is resistance to what is. The constant movement towards future and all the judgments and comparisons of the ego simply keep the ego in place. This keeps non-peace in place.

True peace passes all understanding literally because thought quiets. Life is no longer being lived strictly through the mind. When thought arises, there is no longer identification with or attachment to it. The mind stops searching and seeking. It stops judging, and therefore resisting, others in some vain attempt to define itself. When judgment and resistance arise, they arise in the light of awareness. Thought stops trying to move away from the only place where peace could ever be found: right here, now. Through awareness of not only the thoughts and emotions that cause non-peace but also the mental energy of seeking peace, peace is realized as an attribute of the natural state.

Compassion

The seeker often negotiates with compassion. He gets glimpses of true compassion every now and then when the self falls away for a moment and he sees someone for who they really are on the level of spirit. He sees the suffering in another and knows that it is not real. It is just a story to which consciousness is attaching. He sees that he is not at all separate from the person. Compassion is what is looking in those moments. The self is gone. But then the search to recreate that compassion or the usual thought-based focus on self starts back up, and the self-centeredness obscures compassion again.

When the self gets a hold of compassion, it usurps it for its own gain or tries to make some claim about how it is compassionate. Compassion cannot be created, recreated, or sought after. All of those mental movements obscure the natural compassion within. Compassion is who we are beyond our attempts at seeking it, or recreating past scenarios when it surfaced naturally. The seeker deceives himself into believing that he needs more time or needs to employ some spiritual method to become more compassionate. He does not see that he is negotiating with his own concept again. He creates the illusion that compassion is separate from him and then chases after it.

True compassion exists only in this moment, when the dream of the thought-based self is not obscuring reality, and all searching and seeking towards compassion stops. In presence, compassion is realized as an attribute of the natural state of Oneness.

Freedom

In its sophisticated search, the spiritual ego also negotiates with freedom. It gets stuck in attachment to thought about some life situation, and then seeks to be from free from its own attachment. Therefore, it negotiates with freedom as if to gain something from it. It treats it as a remedy or a fix. But true freedom is not a remedy or fix that one finds by searching for it. Freedom does not exist in the future. Future is not real except as a presently arising thought. So any attempt to seek freedom in the future is bondage to a mental illusion. Freedom is only ever here, now.

When all mental movements towards future, including the movement to find freedom, are seen as illusions, freedom is realized naturally. The separation between self and freedom is created entirely by thought. All negotiations between self and freedom stop in that realization. This is why enlightenment is sometimes referred to as liberation. But the freedom to which the word "liberation" points is not a concept and is not the opposite of bondage. It is the realization that you are the opening in which the concepts of freedom and bondage arise and fall. Seeing yourself as that opening allows you to detach from your own thoughts and from trying to escape one state into another. Liberation is realized in that detachment.

Humility

The ego negotiates with humility, not realizing that humility is simply a word describing the natural state or absence of the ego. During the spiritual search, the seeker may keep a running tab of his negative and positive traits, feeling good about himself when he is balancing these well or when he believes the assets outweigh the liabilities. But true humility never receives its own reward. There is simply no one there to take credit for anything. There is only awareness, watching what is arising now. That awareness is naturally humble.

It wants nothing from life. It is not trying to be someone in relation to someone else. The fullness of life is gained in this realization.

Honesty

The dream self also negotiates with honesty, attempting to tell the truth as best it can as long as the truth does not hurt too much. The ego believes that if it can accumulate enough memories of having told the truth, it will somehow arrive at the destination of "honest person." It is again seeking something in return for its spiritual investment. Self-centeredness is built into that seeking. This concentration on surface level honesty only ignores the deepest lie of all being told—the lie of separation. This deeper lie that the self is separate from the rest of life creates a whole host of surface lies, all designed to strengthen the illusory sense of separateness.

These surface lies involve protecting whatever false self-image is in place. So, the victim tells lies about how life is not treating her fairly, not realizing that the victim story itself is perpetuating separateness and therefore suffering. The wealthy man may tell lies about how money is power while hiding an underlying sense of powerlessness felt by a dream self that cannot find true fulfillment in any amount of money because the separate self is—by its very nature—a story of lack. The artist may be telling lies about how wonderful he is when millions of people buy his music while injecting heroin into his vein, knowing that no amount of fame could ever fulfill his insatiable need for validation, attention, and love. That very insatiability arises from the illusion of separateness.

A husband may tell a lie to himself that his happiness depends on his wife's losing weight, and then lie to his wife when he has an affair, not realizing that his wife's weight was not the problem. He simply believed the painful thought that happiness is somehow outside of himself and dependent on someone else. The guy with a new car may be telling lies about how this piece of metal will somehow enhance his sense of self and his importance in the eyes of others. Someone down on his luck may believe the lie that he does not have everything he needs in this moment, and then may decide to steal from someone else. A terrorist believes the lie that his belief system is the truth, and that others threaten this truth. So he blows himself up in a crowd, not realizing that he made the whole idea of an enemy up in his dream of a separate self. The spiritual seeker may believe that he is more spiritual than others, not realizing that there is no separate self to be spiritual and that the notion that a person can be spiritually "more" or "better" than another person is a dream of self-centered thought, and therefore a lie. The spiritual teacher may tell lies about how she has attained enlightenment, not realizing there is no self to attain enlightenment and that she is separating herself from others by believing that she has something that they do not.

When the deeper lie of a separate self is seen through, most of these surface lies are also seen as illusory, unnecessary, and downright painful. Again, this realization is not about perfection. Lies may still arise in full awareness of this moment. But they will be seen for what they truly are—branches of a much larger tree of deceit, which has its roots in the core lie of the dream of separation.

When All Negotiations Cease

None of this is intended to mean that one should no longer think. When "no self" is realized, thought may still arise. There will just be no attachment to it—no one there to get stuck in it. A higher, more loving intelligence takes over. There is then no seeker left to negotiate with surrender, peace, acceptance, compassion, freedom, honesty and humility. There is no longer the seeking of some benefit from these things, such as a more spiritual self. These spiritual principles are attributes of what is really here—beyond the seeker's ideas about who he is or what he will become.

During the spiritual search, the ego believes it is peeling back layers of an onion to find the true version of itself. In mature spirituality, it is realized that there never was an onion. The onion is the dream.

Thought may resist this entire message. But that which the seeker is beyond the whole movement of seeking knows the truth. There is nothing to grasp. Peace, surrender, joy, freedom, compassion, acceptance, honesty and humility are words within a dream of separation. They are presently arising thoughts that the seeker makes important as part of his dream of becoming. Thought is not the source of true peace, surrender, joy, freedom, compassion, acceptance, honesty and humility. Thought measures, describes, talks, reads, and writes about these things. Only a dream that feels separate from spiritual principles and that seeks something from them would make a big deal out of any of them. When it is realized that these principles are attributes of the natural state, all negotiating ceases. All seeking stops. There is only 'This' and nothing is separate from it. 'This' is naturally peaceful, surrendered, joyful, free, compassionate, accepting, honest, and humble.

Five
NO SELF, NO PATH

Truth is a pathless land . . . it is timeless.

— *J. Krishnamurti*

Every Dream Self is on a Path

There is nothing wrong with having a spiritual path. Every ego has a path because the ego is a path. It is a search. Some consciously travel a spiritual path. Others unconsciously travel a path. The conscious travelers work spiritual programs, meditate, pray, engage in methods, follow teachers and preachers, and belong to communities of other people on similar paths. They are actively and knowingly seeking a better life, a better version of themselves, or God, or the end of self.

The rest are also on a spiritual path, even if they do not realize it. The banker down the road, when working hard for a promotion, is on a spiritual path to become, which is to bring about a better future for himself and his family. Even an addict in the depth of active addiction is on a spiritual path to escape pain and reality, and therefore to bring about something better. The banker and the addict might or might not use the term "spiritual path," but nonetheless they are doing the same thing the conscious travelers are doing. The ego is looking to complete itself in time, in the future.

There is nothing inherently wrong or unhealthy with the mind movement involved in bringing about a better future. In fact, it can be quite healthy. This movement has been critical to the survival of the human species. The reward pathway in the brain is designed to reward us for finding food and sex in order to propagate the species. What could be more loving than going to work each day to make more money in order to feed your kids and put them through school? The suffering occurs when this movement towards future becomes entirely lost in the psychological realm of self. If you are looking for a sense of self in thoughts of future, you are identified with thought. And this is the cause of suffering in humans.

The Manifestations of the Sense of Lack

The path is fueled by an illusory sense of lack. Most people do not directly face the sense of lack within. Instead, it manifests in the most awkward places and times. For example, in the repetitive pushing of slot machine buttons in a casino until you are flat broke. It manifests in the eating of a whole box of Twinkies in one sitting. It manifests as road rage, workaholism, preoccupation with buying the latest gadgets, or constant dieting. The list goes on. All of these manifestations could be summed up as dissatisfaction with what is in this moment.

The sense of lack also reveals itself when you feel that you need a romantic relationship to be happy. It shows up when you find a relationship, but start looking to change the other person or find someone more attractive.

When you are arguing with your spouse and she says something that hurts you deeply, the hurt cuts into your concept of self, which has at its core a sense of lack. This lack is completely an illusion, created by the thought and emotion to which you have attached. It comes directly from an inner attachment to thoughts of past (who you think you are) and thoughts of future (who you want or do not want to become) as well as the emotions that accompany these thoughts. She has attacked that conceptual self, and because you believe falsely that you are what you think, you must fight back with thoughts that hurt her concept of self. In these moments, there is no true relationship or communication. Fear is meeting fear. Lack is meeting lack. Thought is meeting thought. Simply put, a dream is meeting a dream.

On this delicate continuum of time—from past-to-future thoughts—your entire sense of self rests. In fact, the dream self could be described as three realms of thought: thoughts of past, thoughts of future, and thoughts that resist what is occurring in this moment. The dream self is delicate and vulnerable because it is a lie that is obsessed with keeping itself alive and denying the reality of what is. The lie is fueled by the energy of fear. This fear emanates from an inner knowing that true surrender is the end of the ego. The ego sees its own death in that surrender. So, rather than facing this truth, it conjures up an elaborate set of thoughts known as "me."

This self-obsessed path reveals itself in so many destructive ways. Have you noticed that even when you put one vice down, such as cigarettes, another seems to take the place of it, perhaps work, pornography, overeating, exercise, Internet addiction or even spirituality? On this path, only the carrots change. The seeking is always there. Yesterday it was coffee. Today it is Hostess Ding Dongs.

Tomorrow it might be work, a new self-help book, a better sex partner or a new spiritual method. None of these activities are necessarily problematic. Some can even be healthy in the proper perspective. But when you are trying to escape this moment, you are stuck in the insanity of the dream self. The mind is looking for the next playground of becoming so that it does not have to face directly the story of resistance that is arising in this moment.

The ego is constantly busy—doing and becoming within a dream. It is looking for distractions, so that it does not have to face the reality that there is in fact nothing here out of which to make a self. It is running from the true surrender to reality which will swallow its whole dream of becoming. The truth is that there simply is no separate self. To the mind that may sound terrifying. But it is the truth and therefore absolutely liberating. It is the end of suffering. More accurately, it is the realization that suffering was only ever part of the dream of self.

The Pathless Truth

The insanity of becoming is completely hidden to many people. But once it is seen, the door to liberation opens. This seeing is called enlightenment, which simply means to be completely present to whatever is arising now including any movement to escape this moment. Enlightenment is not something reserved for special people or so-called gurus. It does not happen within only one tradition or only in India. It has nothing to do with the term "Advaita Vedanta" or "Buddhism" or even the word "enlightenment." Those are simply pointers. It is available to anyone who is willing to stare directly at the insanity of the constant referencing of past, future, and resistance to now. And when it happens, the sense of a mind-made self is seen as an illusion.

A full awakening includes the waking up out of mind-made concepts such as "Advaita Vedanta," "Buddhism" and "person." In this realization, there is no person or religion there to take credit for the awakening. There is no one there to wake up. So if you hear someone call herself "enlightened" or a "Buddhist," you know it is a dream. The full awakening cannot be realized until there is literally no attachment to any vehicle that may have helped the realization along. Words such as Advaita Vedanta, Buddhism, Christianity, twelve-step fellowship, enlightenment, and God belong to the world of concepts—the world of form. Attachment to the world of form creates suffering and separateness. The words above are beautiful expressions of 'This.' But they are relative truths, little maps pointing to 'This'—the ultimate truth beyond words, beyond form. Spirit itself. Spirit fully realizes itself when the formless awareness looking from your eyes in this moment becomes aware of itself. There must be a jumping off of all form, all concepts. Concepts, no matter how spiritual or fancy they sound, are merely signs pointing beyond themselves to the simple formless awareness that is here right now. The divine is looking through your eyes, seeing itself everywhere.

The realization to which this book points transcends but includes those relative truths. It is the direct seeing that there is a formless realm (discussed more in the chapters *The Inward Depth* and *the Space of Love*) which gives birth to this realm of form. The realms of form (i.e., words, concepts, beliefs) and formlessness (i.e., space or awareness) are not at all separate but are in fact two ways of looking at one reality. 'This.' When you get lost in ideas, concepts, and beliefs, you are lost in the realm of form and denying the formless realm. This is a denial of the very truth to which the word God points. The words God and 'This' are pointing to this ultimate truth that cannot be grasped by an intellect that is lost in the dualism of concepts. Concepts are merely maps pointing to the direct experience of the reality known as life in this moment.

The truth is whatever is arising now and the realization that it is not arising to any person or in any religion or tradition or along any path. In truth, life is just happening. The dream is the belief that life is happening to you and that you are on a spiritual path.

Spiritual awakening is a pathless truth. There is no path to being awake because beingness is already awake. The awakening is realized when there is openness to what is in this moment. It cannot come about through time, effort, control or searching. There is nothing you can do to get there, in terms of effort, because awakeness is already here. It is what is reading these words. It is what is breathing. In fact, any effort to find awakeness obscures the realization of what is already here, in the timeless. All you have to do is notice and that takes no effort at all.

Life simply moves freely. You are that freedom. The freedom occurs only in the absence of the time-bound path. The path is such a heavy burden of mental self to carry around. When you believe an illusion, you welcome the suffering that comes with it. The truth cannot be found on the path, because the path is only a presently arising thought. The truth is what is looking at that presently arising idea. You are the truth. In that realization, suffering ends.

True peace passes all conceptual understanding, and can only be found when all attempts at trying to understand it conceptually or find it in time fall away. The mind is wonderful. What a brilliant tool! Cherish it. Use it for practical matters. But it is not who you are. And it will obscure this peace if you truly believe that it can tell you who you are, or what life, truth, or God is. Thought is not interested in this moment. It is doing the best it can to avoid 'This.' It knows that this moment is its end.

When you are ninety years old on your deathbed, the question may arise as to why it feels like you spent a life of becoming. You might wonder why you never got "there." You might realize that you would not have recognized "there" even if you had arrived, because the mind kept changing the carrots, kept changing what "there" would or should look like. And you may or may not realize on your deathbed that you were always "here." You were here—in the only moment where life ever happens. Ultimately, enlightenment is about waking up to that truth right now. The path is obscuring the truth. The path is simply thought projecting a sort of virtual reality of constant becoming. When the rat steps off the wheel, he laughs hysterically, realizing that he made the whole idea of a wheel up.

If anything, "enlightenment" is pointing to the absence of reaching towards anything called "enlightenment." Or stated another way, it is the realization that you were only ever reaching for your own thoughts, which were arising now. Insane, isn't it? You realize that "enlightenment" is just an idea arising now, as is the notion of "you." So the word "enlightenment" is pointing to the complete stepping out of the self-centered dream that there is a "you" on a "path" to "enlightenment." When the dream dies, you see the whole. You see 'This.' You realize you are not separate from 'This' despite all your efforts to separate yourself through thought. You see all thoughts about 'This' are simply arising in 'This.' The seeking and the finding arise and fall in 'This.' 'This' does not answer every question that gave rise to the illusion of a path. It merely makes them not matter. You realize that 'This' is what you were seeking on the illusory path.

The Wisdom of Noticing

There is a principle which is a bar against all information, which is proof against all arguments and which cannot fail to keep a man in everlasting ignorance—that principle is contempt prior to investigation.

– Herbert Spencer

Six
INQUIRY: THE OPENING INTO THE ONE

The unwillingness to actually see what causes your suffering is what keeps your mind bound in cycles of suffering. Are you willing to see what causes your suffering? If so, then you are willing for everything to change. . . Yes, it is a radical notion. This is where most people start backing away.

— Gangaji

Noticing Thought

Don't let the fancy title of this chapter fool you. Remember, awakening is not a future event. It is a present seeing. And "Oneness" is not a belief system or experience. It is not an event in time. You are not on a path towards anything including spiritual awakening, Oneness, happiness, contentment, or freedom. These words are merely pointing to the present recognition of inseparability, to the seeing that there are no separate things in life. This means there is no separate "you." In that present realization, the sense of being cut off or separate from life disappears. Wholeness is realized. All lines of division are seen through. Paradoxically, it is only then that perfect freedom and contentment are realized.

One could say, then, that there is no one to do any inquiry. But that puts the cart before the horse. If you are reading this book, chances are you take yourself to be a separate person. Inquiry can assist you in seeing through that sense of separation. So the word "opening" is referring to the decision you make as an apparently separate person to look at your present experience and find out why separation feels real in this very moment, why you are suffering, seeking or in conflict with life and others. Why are you on a path towards anything in the future when life only happens now? Like all methods, inquiry, when it has fulfilled its purpose, falls away. What is left is the sweetness of inseparability. This inseparability is what you've been seeking, even though you may not have known this.

In this moment, you may not really see thought. You think you do, but not the kind of seeing called "inquiry." People normally investigate a thought by thinking additional, related thoughts, which appear to evaluate earlier thoughts. This is analytical thinking, important for practical aspects of life (e.g. work, programming software, fixing the car), but an obstacle to enlightenment or self-realization, as it is sometimes called. Analytical thinking leads to the never ending succession of thoughts streaming through your head. Over ninety percent of that is useless, repetitive, and self-centered. When I say "inquiry," I am not referring to that stream of thought. I am referring to that which notices it. "Inquiry" is not a new method or path to enlightenment. It is that which sees all methods and paths. It is presence, but it also carries with it intelligence because insight is gained from the inward looking. That insight is constantly revealing that there is no such thing as a separate self, and that separateness is an illusion created by thought.

The term "inquiry" is referring to true intelligence or awareness, which is noticing that stream of thought in each moment, and how it creates the illusion of separation. To investigate thought with inquiry means to allow each thought to arise in full awareness and to no longer assume each thought is even true or real or that it requires a response or action at all. This is true self-awareness.

J. Krishnamurti spoke to this true intelligence:

> *The more we think over a problem, the more we . . . analyze, and discuss it, the more complex it becomes. So is it possible to look at the problem comprehensively, wholly? How is this possible? Because that, it seems to me, is our major difficulty. Our problems are being multiplied—there is imminent danger of war, there is every kind of disturbance in our relationships—and how can we understand all that comprehensively, as a whole? Obviously, it can be solved only when we can look at it as a whole—not in compartments, not divided. When is that possible? Surely, it is only possible when the process of thinking—which has its source in the "me," the self, in the background of tradition, of conditioning, of prejudice, of hope, of despair—has come to an end. Can we understand this self, not by analyzing, but by seeing the thing as it is, being aware of it as a fact and not as a theory—not seeking to dissolve the self in order to achieve a result but seeing the activity of the self, the "me," constantly in action?*

To inquire is to look inward at what is arising, rather than assuming that all of your thoughts, which are outward interpretations of the world, are true. It is to see the mind-made self (ego), and to realize what, if anything, is beyond or prior to, or inclusive of that. Ramana Maharshi often spoke of the self-inquiry in which one asks what the source of the "I" thought is. This is an asking inwardly, to realize the True Self, beyond ego. If this works for you, use it. If you look within to find the source of the thought "I am" and you bump into a beautiful emptiness in which everything is arising, that is it. You have found the truth of who you are.

For those who do not become instantly self-realized through Ramana's inquiry-style, consider this: to inquire also means to see the activity of the self in action in each moment. It means to notice each thought, from that bundle of thoughts known as "me," as it arises and falls within your field of awareness, rather than to blindly engage each thought with analysis and internal discussion. When the conceptual mind first reads that it may think that inquiry is completely self-centered, focusing on self all the time. No. This is the door to the end of self-centeredness. Whether you are aware of it or not, self-centered thoughts are polluting everything you do. Inquiry is just noticing that, so that the true quietness of who you really are can be realized.

This bundle of thoughts known as ego is made up of thoughts of past, future, and resistance to what is happening now. This is your thought world, and it is trying desperately to resist acceptance of what is in this moment, to escape reality. As Eckhart Tolle says: "Whenever you are immersed in compulsive thinking, you are avoiding what is. You don't want to be where you are. Here, Now."

But do not believe anyone who tells you these things, including me. When you begin watching thoughts, you notice for yourself this insanity playing out—this resistance to peace. You begin to notice that one thought leads to another, which leads to another. It is endless. Most, if not all, thoughts are assumed to be true, necessary, and real. They are rarely questioned or even seen. You believe the whole story streaming through your head. You are at its mercy. You wake up in the morning, and before long, thoughts of what you must do for the day rush in, one after another: "I must talk to my boss when I get to work;" "I should eat at Rojo's Restaurant for lunch;" "I have to pick up my child from school;" "I'm too fat, I need to diet;" "Tonight I need to clean the bathroom." In the moment when each of these thoughts arises, if it arises in full awareness, you see that you do not need to analyze life in this way. You see that this repetitive stream of thoughts is by its very nature self-centered. All you ever do is think about yourself. Do not make a problem out of that. Simply notice it.

You do not need to use this repetitive stream of thought in order to live life. Life simply happens. It lives through you. Sure, some practical planning for the day may be needed. But the psychological attachment to thought is so often divorced from practicality that it is a nuisance. Analysis itself becomes paralyzing, so much so that people live almost exclusively "in their heads," unable to take clear action. Thought keeps clear, focused action from taking place. But do not walk away having formulated a belief that thought keeps clear action from happening. This truth is directly accessible through your own inward noticing.

Instead of believing what spiritual teachers are saying, I gently invite you to investigate what is happening in your own head and in your emotional body in each moment. I invite you to look at each and every movement of self, inside the mind. Look at how you seek approval, attention, praise, or acknowledgment from others. In those moments, you are actually watching your own self-centeredness, your need to gain something from others—to be a more complete you.

Notice each and every judgment of people and situations that arises in your mind. By watching all judgments, this mental outward pointing towards "others" is seen as false. The mind naturally quiets when you see that judgment is simply an attempt, through comparison, to define and strengthen the egoic little separate "me." Outward judgment comes straight from inward insecurity. If your mind does not quiet in the noticing of outward judgment and inward insecurity, watch the thought which says it should be quiet. That thought is the insanity of becoming, keeping the quietness from being realized.

Watch the presently arising thoughts that tell you that something that happened or did not happen in your past affects who you are in this moment. That is just a story. Notice the presently arising thoughts that tell you that something needs to happen in the future for you to be at peace, or find freedom, happiness or acceptance. Peace, freedom, happiness and acceptance happen only now, when there is complete awareness of these stories of past and future.

Watch as your mind seeks certainty. It seeks to be right, to know, to conclude, to put to rest, and to resolve. And yet it never fully and finally resolves anything. The mind believes that, through conceptual understanding (analysis), it will find rest in a more complete sense of self. But it cannot rest this way, not truly. Each conclusion is as shaky and temporary as a mountain made of dry sand. There is always another conclusion, opinion, counterpoint waiting to destroy the original conclusion.

Conclusions kill the spirit. They smother the noticing. They result in a false sense of certainty and security. Conclusions carry with them a "closing off" energy. Awareness stops looking at what is in the moment conclusions are formed. Anything that shuts off awareness is false. This does not mean that you should never conclude anything. You must make conclusions at work and in certain other practical areas of life. This is not about the suppression of anything including the suppression of conclusions. This is about noticing.

Notice that conclusions, when there is attachment to them, become the weapons of argument, disagreement, debate, conflict, religion, and war. Conclusions are the building blocks of the dream self. My conclusion bumps up against your contrary conclusion. My attachment collides into your attachment. There is no true meeting then. No true relationship. In this collision of wills, we are not looking at a problem together. We are only interested in maintaining our "rightness," our conclusions. We are only interested in maintaining ego, which is separation and conflict. The energy behind agreement and disagreement is the energy of ego itself.

To inquire means to be aware of all movements of self whenever they arise. These movements are directed towards one aim—keeping self-centeredness alive. Inquiry means to see conclusion, debate, conflict, argument, agreement, disagreement, religion, and war as essentially just one movement of self, arising in different forms or with different degrees of energy. This movement seeks to create, strengthen, and confirm the dream of separation.

Perhaps you are saying to yourself, "How is agreement egoic?" When you inquire within, you see that when you seek agreement with another on the level of mind, you are often seeking confirmation of what you already know and believe. The ego is essentially a set of thoughts about who you are, including what you know and believe about life. Again, there is nothing wrong with thoughts or beliefs. But if you believe that thought can tell you who you are, or what life or God is, then you are living in delusion. Therefore, any over-reliance on thinking feeds the dream of separation. In agreement, who you think you are gets mirrored back to you, by someone else who holds your same view or opinion on the particular subject. That is fine. Seek agreement to your heart's desire. There is nothing particularly unhealthy about agreement. I am referring here to the energy of seeking for it. Do not deceive yourself. Notice that the seeking of agreement is the seeking of confirmation of who you think you are. You are seeking confirmation of the tape recording of memory within you. This is often on such an unconscious level that people do not notice. This seeking is not openness. It is not true intelligence where you are able to see all sides of a problem. Notice that when you set out to find an answer to some problem or solution, quite often you have a preconceived notion of what answer or solution you want to find. Your actions and thoughts are geared in the direction of your already-established conclusions. In this way, you are not truly looking for a solution. You are looking to confirm your own preconceived notion. You are therefore deceiving yourself and others. Do you see the self-centeredness inherent in this?

The invitation to inquire is not an invitation to suppress your beliefs or thoughts, or to no longer express them. This invitation is simply pointing to an entirely different, more loving energy than that which emanates from human interaction that is stuck on the level of the mind. This more loving energy emanates naturally from the noticing. What is noticing is love itself.

Noticing Emotion

Inquiry includes watching closely what arises and falls within your emotional body. Be very curious about whatever negative emotion is arising in your body in the moment it arises. Let it arise within your awareness. Feel feelings directly as soon as they arise. Take your awareness into the emotion, and inhabit it from the inside out. Also, notice the space around the emotion. Notice that every emotion arises within the space of who you are. Do not label emotions "fear" or "anger" or tell stories about how they should or should not be here. Do not try to rationalize, justify or think them away. If labeling, storytelling, rationalization, and justification arise, watch these movements also.

Face emotions directly for what they are—energy movements within your body. Making a self out of what is arising just strengthens the dream. When you investigate emotion in this way, you realize that emotions are simply letting you know that your thoughts are self-centered. So watch the corresponding story in your head when emotions arise in the body. It is a story all about you, and how you are not getting what you want, or how you do not want what you have. Inquiry is a moment by moment looking inward at these stories and movements, and seeing that they make up a psychological loop that feeds on itself, always and only concerned with its own self-definition and separation. This loop keeps you in a dream that you are the center of life.

It is insane to ever want something to be other than the way it is. This argument with reality keeps the dream self at the center. Anger, fear, jealousy, hurt, envy, greed, anxiety, sadness, and resentment are all versions of non-peace. Resistance to any of these emotions is also non-peace. Resistance to a negative emotion is the only thing that would ever want that emotion to go away. So when you desire for anger to go away or to be something other than what it is, you are applying non-peace to non-peace. This is the insanity of becoming. By trying to seek a future state of non-anger, you are avoiding the anger that is arising now. You are avoiding reality. The avoidance or resistance to any negative emotions, including anger, fear, jealousy, hurt, envy, greed, anxiety, sadness, or resentment only increases the energy behind these emotions. Inquiry means to watch any story, on an emotional or mental level, which says that whatever energy is arising now should not be arising. Be completely with whatever emotion is arising now.

Inquiry is looking inward. Through looking inward, it is seen that all is One. I do not mean "One" as some conclusion, belief, or mental certainty, but rather as an ongoing questioning and openness to what is. Inquiry does not involve doing anything. There is no becoming to inquiry. One does not inquire to get anything out of it. To inquire means to be naturally open to what is already happening, to notice the movement of becoming already playing out within the mental dream. Notice that there is no one there inquiring. There is only openness. This openness sees and questions all conclusions, beliefs, mental certainty, emotions, stories, movements, and reactions. Then action is taken from that openness—not from analysis, story, ego, and separation. Thus, action is no longer self-centered. It is taken on account of the whole. Stated another way, once the story of self is seen thoroughly, it dissolves. God can then take action through you. One need do nothing but inquire. This dream self cannot be dissolved through self-will. It must dissolve on its own. Just notice. The truth takes over from there.

Seven
THE STORY OF UNCONSCIOUSNESS

To be conscious is not a mystical or special ability reserved only for gurus. It simply means to "see" why you suffer. Seeing is always a present activity. No one becomes conscious in the future. Look at the story you are believing presently. To be unconscious is to not see why you suffer right now. And suffering is always because you choose a story over present seeing itself.

— *Scott Kiloby*

What does unconsciousness mean as a spiritual term? Most of us think of what Wikipedia describes as "a dramatic alteration of one's mental state that involves complete or near-complete lack of responsiveness to people and other environmental stimuli." We refer to unconsciousness as what happens, for example, when someone gets "knocked out" due to a blow to the head or is completely unresponsive as a result of illness or coma.

Spiritual unconsciousness is perhaps not as severe as the unresponsiveness one experiences from being "out cold" due to a blow to the head by a blunt object, but in many respects it is very much "a dramatic alteration of one's mental state that involves complete or near-complete lack of responsiveness to people and other environmental stimuli."

Spiritually, humans are unconscious or ignorant of who they are and what they are doing. "Ignorant" is not used here as some derogatory slang term. I am speaking of the literal sense of the word as "to be unaware of the fact of something." In its most basic sense, unconsciousness means "not seeing" what is arising in this moment. In the egoic state, humans are not aware of what is arising within including thought, emotions, and reactions. Instead, thought, emotions, and reactions are injecting self-centeredness into every move and every action. This unconscious attempt at control is resistance itself. In this way, a person or ego could be defined as resistance to what is arising. Resistance is the root of suffering. Thus, enlightenment and presence are words that describe what is happening when resistance and control are absent. What is happening is life, unencumbered by the self-centered energy of resistance.

One Must See for Oneself

You can read about the world's religions all you want. You can learn the definition of sin in Christianity. You can read what Buddha meant by suffering. There are tons of books on Maya, or the veil of delusion in Hinduism. You can attend a local twelve-step meeting where they will be discussing human "defects" that can cause harm. But the texts and teachers of these or any traditions can only take you so far. Ultimately, they are pointing to the unconsciousness within your own mind. So, one must see for oneself in order to be free from the illusory suffering caused by this unconsciousness.

First, one must see that the mind is unconscious. Unconsciousness has also been referred to as the human ego, or as self-centeredness. You may understand conceptually that thought is self-centered, but that is not enough. Another thought in your mind that says, "My thought is self-centered," hardly goes far in allowing you to see the actual fact of self-centeredness as it arises in each moment.

The awareness in you is the only "thing" that will truly see the self-centered nature of thought. Awareness is "that within you which sees" not "that which is seen." Thoughts are forms or objects that arise within you. Thought is that which is seen. Awareness is much closer, much simpler, and far more humble. It is that which sees the arising and falling of all thoughts, including even thoughts about awareness. Thinking about presence is not presence. It is just another story. Watch the story "become present" or "be more present." That is a story of becoming. Presence is only ever here now. There is no becoming to it.

You already know what it means to see unconsciousness. Have you ever been driving down the road for miles without the conscious awareness that you are driving down the road? All of a sudden, you snap out of it and realize that you were deep in thought. Had you been fully aware of that stream of thought, you would have noticed that it was mostly self-centered in nature. You were judging, comparing, referring back to the past, projecting into the future, or resisting something that was arising in the moment. All these movements of thought contain at the center a sense of "me." In your head, it is all about you.

Even if you were thinking about others while driving, those thoughts were essentially all about you, including how those others relate to you, whether they are doing what you want them to do, and who you are in relation to them. Please do not believe or disbelieve me. Do not start philosophizing in your head about whether I am right or wrong about this, and whether your thought is truly self-centered. Agreeing or disagreeing with someone else's conception simply reinforces your own memory—what you learned from the past, or in some other book, or who you think you are. The reinforcement of memory is self-centered. Look for yourself, now, in this moment, at what is arising, whether you are driving down the road, doing the laundry, or reading this book.

This veil of thought does not just occur on the road. It is your constant companion. You may notice it more while driving because of the inherent danger of not paying attention while driving. But most people live life in each moment behind this same veil of thought. In the unconscious state, when you talk to people, you are often talking only to the image of a person in your head, an image made up of a set of thoughts or attributes you have assigned to the person based upon their past actions or inactions. This is not who they are. You are interacting only with your own mental image of the person, not with the person. They are often doing the same thing to you. Byron Katie said, "No two people have ever met." This is what she was pointing to—one image relating to another image. No true relationship or meeting happens when an image is meeting an image. This is the dream of separation.

To be conscious is "to see" thought, which means to notice that you are living behind this cloud of thinking in each moment. Watch how thought comes to meet everything—from a flower, to a sidewalk, to your aunt, and to your job. You are thinking life, not living it. Thinking is largely resistance. You are resisting the reality of what is, in favor of your own thought-based interpretation. This resistance creates the illusion of suffering and conflict. But there simply is no suffering or conflict outside the dream of thought. So you are dreaming your own pain into existence.

Emotional Unconsciousness

In the unconscious state, emotions also arise "in the dark" so to speak. Your awareness does not see them in the moment they arise. The term "I saw red" refers to emotional unconsciousness where someone gets very angry, and essentially loses complete sight of what he is doing, sometimes resulting in harm to someone else verbally or physically. Only after the fact does the person look back and realize he was not conscious during the heated moment. But the sense of "seeing red" is simply a description of a state that rests on one end of a full spectrum of emotional unconsciousness. The slightest irritation or uneasiness, if unwatched as it arises in the moment, has the capacity to turn into a self-centered resentment.

These energy forms we call "emotions" arise and fall in varying degrees and flavors throughout the day. In the unconscious state, you do not fully face these emotions. Instead, your mind begins to tell stories about the feelings. For example, a thought of future arises, and a corresponding fear is felt in the chest and stomach.

Instead of allowing awareness to become directly aware of the feeling of fear in the body, you think more thoughts about why you should or should not be feeling fear, you try to justify and rationalize the fear, or you analyze possible future scenarios and outcomes in some attempt to get rid of the fear. This entire movement of thought is an attempt to escape fear. Thought is keeping you from feeling the fear directly, and allowing it to come into the light of awareness. You are telling a story which is resisting the fear. This story of resistance fuels the fear, which in turn fuels the story, which in turn fuels the fear. You are then stuck in the cycle of suffering, created entirely by a dream. In the moments when this happens, turn your attention directly on the fear and watch any mental story which arises in resistance to it.

Enlightened Unconsciousness

You can bury yourself in spiritual books all you want. Go to church, to twelve-step meetings, to synagogues, to mosques, to Sanghas. Do all those things. They are wonderful. Enjoy them. Be in spiritual community with others. But ultimately, if you are not aware of what is arising now in your body and mind, you will continue in the state of unconsciousness. The story may change. You may go from being a seeker to an "enlightened being." You may tell others how conscious or present or spiritual you are or are becoming, or how close to God you have become—all because you have read so many books, gone to so many church services, or been a Sangha member for so long.

You may repeat fancy spiritual sayings and believe that you have attained this or that level of enlightenment.

But if you do not see the story you are telling, you will remain unconscious. I call this "enlightened unconsciousness." The story of the "spiritual seeker who found enlightenment" is the last and final dream that dies in the light of the truth. It is the last story to go. If you believe you are enlightened or a spiritual teacher, reality will come around to smack you in the face in one way or another. Suffering arises when you believe lies and all stories are lies, no matter how grand or awful they are.

Enlightenment cannot be grasped by the mind. When the mind gets a hold of it, it turns it into a story of self, belief, or mental position. It strips away the truth to which the word "enlightenment" points. Enlightenment is not reserved for gurus or available only after years of practice or seeking either. It is your birthright. It is not a special state, experience, thought, or emotion that one has to find or maintain. It is not an idea to grasp. True enlightenment is love itself. It is presence. It is the seeing that, before you think anything about a self, other, or the world, there is only non-conceptual presence. And that non-conceptual presence naturally and effortlessly allows everything to be just as it is, every idea, emotion, state, sensation, experience, and object.

This is not a love you can own in your story. Love does not say "I am enlightened." Only a dream self trying to be someone in relation to someone else would say that. That is separation. Love is non-separation. In truth, there is simply no one there. And no separate objects. Although you think there is a self, that self is nothing more than a series of arisings, a series of thoughts, emotions, sensations, states, and experiences that happen one after the other. It is only the mind that makes those arisings into separate objects. The main object is the ego, or self. That object can never know enlightenment. A good word for enlightenment is humility. In the absence of the dream self, there is humility, but no one claiming to be humble. The word "humility" points to your absence as the center of life. Enlightenment is realized only in the absence of your stories, which means in the total surrender to whatever is arising in this moment.

Rest as non-conceptual awareness as often as possible. That is the key to freedom, the secret within this book. And when you realize non-conceptual awareness as your real identity, notice that it allows the entire world to be just as it is (including every thought, emotion, state, sensation, and experience). See that the world cannot appear without awareness. They are fundamentally inseparable.

Eight
SELF-REALIZATION

An inquiry is not a teaching. It does not seek to answer or teach anything. It merely looks, playing in the truth of curiosity like a child discovering a seashell for the first time without any notion that this thing in his hand is called a "seashell."

— Scott Kiloby

Self-realization is a fancy and somewhat confusing term. Let's demystify it. It simply means to find out if there is anything about you that is not a story. Is there anything there beyond thought? Let's look.

Thought Is of the Past

Thought is of the past. Is it not? Look inward. Thought is memory. Even the conclusion that thought is of the past is a conclusion carried through time, which means held in the mind as memory. The fact that I restate that insight here does not make it fresh or new.

Is all thought of the past? I sit back in my chair and stop typing. But before that last sentence was formed, the actual event of "sitting back in my chair and stopping typing" occurred. Thought is playing a game of catch-up with the present moment. It is lagging behind, describing the past. This moment is fleeting, absolutely temporary.

Even when thought is describing what is happening now, the concepts it uses are of the past. At some point in the past, the brain memorized certain concepts such as the concept of "I," the concept of "chair," and the concepts of "sitting," "stopping," and "typing." These words are not that which they describe. They are a story, based on memorized concepts, of an unknowable reality called "life" happening in this moment. Concepts are never the truth. They are only ever telling a story about the truth. Thought is a dream. It is memory. Past.

Life is like a great jazz improv. It moves, wherever it moves, in its own mysterious way in the timeless present. Thought is like a music theorist, following the jazz artist around, writing down the notes that are played in some attempt to understand and explain it. Life cannot be understood that way. It cannot be comprehended fully or clearly through thought and interpretation. The past (thought) will never see this moment the way it really is.

Are thoughts of future also of the past? If I say, "I hope this happens tomorrow" or "I do not want that to happen next week," I must know whether the happening or not happening of the event will be good or bad. I must have some idea as to whether I will prefer the event to happen or not happen. In order for me to know that, I must consult thought, which is past. I must have some memory in my head of whether a happening will or will not be desirable, perhaps a past experience or an idea which someone has persuaded me to believe.

Memory is constantly projecting itself into what appears to be the future. But the projection is just an appearance. In truth, the past is projecting itself forward into a dream of thought called "future." I cannot truly see the future. So any projection which is seen is a dream of thought, which means past. Thought is a loop in that way. It is past, appearing as "future." And when that future event happens or does not happen, I make a judgment about whether it is in fact a desirable event. And that judgment becomes memory. It becomes part of this thought-based self called ego. Do you see this loop? The ego is the loop. As long as I consult only that loop, I am consulting only thought. I am therefore living in a conceptual dream, rather than in the reality of this moment.

This is the inquiry that J. Krishnamurti enjoyed, "whether thought is of the past." But this inquiry is not something one learns in a book or from some teacher. It must be taken inward and looked at with the innocence of a child. No effort can be applied to this looking. Effort seeks to move forward. It is energy that is trying to escape what is. It is trying to get or achieve something from the looking, which implies future. Therefore, it is not completely present to what is in this moment.

To see what is in this moment, there must be effortlessness and innocence. One must realize the truth for himself, like the child discovering the seashell without any notion that this thing is called a "seashell." I must discover the nature of the thing myself, by looking at it, not thinking about it. When I think about the object, I am only projecting memory onto it. I am only projecting the past onto it. I cannot trust another to tell me what this object is. I must not blindly trust spiritual teachers, or spiritual books, all of which are putting ideas in my mind. I must question each one of those ideas, *not* with the analytical mind, but with awareness itself. These ideas, if they do not arise within awareness, become my memory, which projects itself forward into a future dream. I then go searching for truth only within my own thoughts, which is self-centered and ignorant. I will not find the truth that way. I will only find my own memory, which is merely a set of ideas planted in my mind by others. If I do not see this self-centered loop of thought, I remain stuck in it. I remain stuck in ignorance.

In order to see what is true, I must stand alone, and look at what is truly here, in this moment, beyond these thoughts of what is here. This moment is always telling the truth. Thought will not show me this moment, only awareness will. In order to see beyond the mind's ignorance, I must be fully aware of the ideas that have been planted in my mind—the programming. I must see these thoughts as they arise. The programming enslaves me to thought—to myself. Without awareness of these ideas as they play out, I become addicted to thought and therefore addicted to self.

Can you take this inquiry inward? Digest it, but not analytically. Just look at it. See whether thought is of the past. See for yourself in each moment.

Who Am I?

This "I" is a concept. It is past. It must be because it is thought. Without thought there is no "me." With thought comes "me." So "I" am the past. I am a thought. And since thought is a dream of what is, I am a dream.

If I am only a dream, who is asking all this? Thought cannot answer that. If someone tells the child that what he is holding is a seashell, it does not mean that he now knows what the object is. He has only learned a thought, which he has placed onto the object. The child cannot truly know the depth of it through thought. I cannot know who I truly am through thought.

Thought never touches the actuality of what is. Thought has never been here, in this moment. It never touches this moment—the actual events happening now. So to live life through thought is literally to live this moment only through a conceptual dream of past. Yet thought arises even now. So what is it that is looking at the thought that is arising now? There is something deeper than this "I" thought, and all other thoughts. That is who I truly am. I am an actuality. There is a conscious, alive, intelligent, loving beingness here in this moment watching all these thoughts as they arise. I am that, whatever that is.

Am I Separate from the Rest of Life?

Is this consciousness which I truly am separate from the rest of life? These are not fingers typing. This is not "inquiry." There is no one here named Scott Kiloby. That is all a story of thought. Life is one inseparable reality in the now. Thus, there is no "me" here separate from the rest of what is occurring. There is no separation, spatially, until the story of mind begins, which is the dream.

There is nothing that can be seen as an ending or a beginning either. The concepts of ending and beginning are of the past. They exist only in time, which is mind. Thus, there is no separation temporally, except through thought. There is only the timeless present.

I am therefore not separate from life. So I must step into a dream of thought in order to be a "separate" me.

But even the notions of "stepping in" or "stepping out" are part of the dream of separation, as are ideas such as "this moment" or "the past" or "dream." This is all of the past, and not of this moment. The conceptual is only ever pointing to the actual. But it can never truly see the actual for what it is—a mystery.

There is consciousness here, in this moment. But even that is a story. Thought sometimes arises, as the content of consciousness. But to even conclude that content is somehow separate from consciousness is itself thought, which is past. Content is therefore not separate from consciousness. Form is not separate from formlessness. Only thought makes "content" and "consciousness" or "form" and "formlessness" separate. Thought is the only "thing" that would make two here, when there is only One. There is only 'This.' And thought is the only "thing" which would even care about whether something is separate from something else.

Can I Become Enlightened or Liberated?

Can I become enlightened? Thought projects past into future, looking for the end of itself, which it imagines to be enlightenment. Enlightenment is part of the dream. There is no self to find enlightenment. When I place a word such as "enlightenment" on this self, it is only my memory coming to describe what is in this moment. When I look for myself in the future, I am only chasing my own thought, my own past. I will never find the truth through an idea. I will only find the idea. So the idea that "I" can become "enlightened" or "self-realized" is a dream of thought. There is a truth beyond this dream of thought. That is the deeper truth to which the word "enlightenment" points. But I will never reach that. It is realized only in the absence of the idea of a separate me. It is realized when the dream of me is seen for what it is—an illusion.

Can I become liberated? Thought only ever meets its own projection. It is a self-centered, psychological loop. Only thought would want to step out of the loop or find liberation. Only thought would want to step out of itself or find the end of self. So if there is an end to this mind-made me, it will not be realized through thought. It will be realized through presence, through noticing what is in this moment. This includes noticing whatever thought is arising now. Thought conjures up a thing called "liberation" and seeks to reach its own creation. That is not liberation. That is just another idea. True liberation is beyond attachment to thought. It sees thought. It is the beingness which is in this moment, and which sees the entire, futile dream that a person could ever become liberated. Liberation is realized when the self stops chasing after it. A dream cannot find a dream.

To say that, within this One Life, there is something here or over there, which is a "person" who is "liberated" or "enlightened" is the dream talking. So I cannot place my trust in those who call themselves liberated or enlightened. They are dreaming. I must look inward. Only inward looking will show me the truth. It will show me that separation is a dream of thought. So the idea that there is a separate person who is or can become enlightened or liberated is a mind-created dream. The repetition of non-duality or other spiritual teachings, imposed by teachers, is merely reinforcing ideas about enlightenment and liberation. It is reinforcing the memory within me—the dream self. The truth cannot be found in ideas or beliefs. I cannot blindly believe ideas coming from the mouths of others. Ideas can be taken as pointers, but they must be questioned as to whether they are absolutely true. One must stand alone, and investigate and inquire within. In this investigation, the very idea that I can become enlightened or liberated is watched. In that watching, awareness expands and swallows this dream called "me." There is literally no one there inquiring. The mind quiets. It is then realized that this thing I call consciousness or beingness is already liberated. It is already enlightened. This "me"—with all its self-centeredness and obsession with thought—has merely been obscuring this reality.

I cannot answer the question, "What is here beyond the dream of me?" with any mental certainty. I do not know. Some deeper "I" that cannot be named is here. Call it God or Oneness. "Love" feels closer to the truth. In any event, the mind cannot grasp it, no matter what word is used. Mental certainty is a dream. Not knowing is the real wisdom. Wisdom cannot be fooled or deceived by thought.

When the child is told that this thing in his hand is called a "seashell," will he foolishly claim to know it then or will he still see it for the mystery it truly is? Seeing life as the mystery it is allows awareness to expand. Awareness is a deeper intelligence than thought. It sees the depth of something, rather than just the name or the surface only. Awareness sees life without the veil of self-centered mental interpretation. Yet the only "thing" that would make awareness or thought more important than the other is another thought. Enlightenment is not about ending thought or living in pure awareness. It is dualistic to ever want to push any aspect of 'This' away in favor of some other aspect. Enlightenment is realizing that it all arises in 'This.' 'This' welcomes awareness and thought, pushing nothing away. 'This' is at one with whatever is arising. But 'This' is never fooled about the truth, which is that attachment to thought keeps the "me" locked in ignorance.

Thought is not the problem. It never was. A problem can only be found in attachment to thought. Since all thought is a dream of past, there is only ever attachment to an illusion. In reality, there is no problem. There is only 'This.'

$\mathscr{N}ine$
THE MYTH OF ACCEPTANCE

A glimpse of the true nature of your being is like a kiss from the divine. The kiss itself is a mystery of grace. There is nothing you could have done to create it.

— Gangaji

Have you ever deceived yourself into believing that you need to become more accepting or learn to accept life or yourself more? Acceptance is not a learning game. You do not accumulate acceptance over time. Acceptance does not happen in the future. It happens now or not at all.

The spiritual search occurs when you believe presently arising thoughts that tell you that something should be happening other than what is happening now. The mental strategy of wanting to become more accepting or learning to accept life or yourself more places acceptance in time, in the future. It places it in thought. But thought cannot see this moment, which is the only place where acceptance can happen. Instead of engaging in some belief about how you are becoming more accepting or some mental strategy to bring about acceptance in some future moment, notice the arising of that belief or strategy now. The belief or strategy is an attempt to escape this moment and place acceptance in time, which means in the mind. Escape into thought (into time) is not acceptance. In fact, by its very nature, it is non-acceptance (non-seeing) of what is arising now. What is arising now is the belief or mental strategy.

In noticing the belief or strategy, you are present. True acceptance is a mystery of grace. There is nothing you can do to create it. Noticing non-acceptance of what is in this moment is true acceptance. There is no doing involved. No self.

Acceptance Is Not Found in Time

The notion of "coming to acceptance" implies time, and time is thought. You are attached to some projected outcome in your illusory search to be more accepting. Simply put, you are identifying with a presently arising thought about a fictitious future "you." It is fictitious because it is only thought. You are dreaming about some future state of acceptance and trying to convince yourself that you need to reach that state or are reaching that state. This is perfectly designed to keep self-centeredness in place. You get to keep the focus on you—about how you are not quite there yet, but you are getting there. Acceptance does not happen in time—in the mind. Thought does not accept. Thought merely changes the particular story the dream self is telling. Thought measures, comments, judges, dreams, compares, replays, resists, convinces, and analyzes a situation. It does not truly accept anything. Thought can dream about future acceptance or rehash the ways in which it was or was not able to accept past situations, but it cannot truly accept anything now because it is a dream of time. I am not encouraging you to stop thinking about acceptance. You could not even if you tried. I am just asking whether you notice the insanity to which these words are pointing.

Acceptance happens when you are aware of thought. It occurs naturally when you are aware not only of the thoughts that argue with reality, but also of the entire mental movement to become more accepting in time. That becoming energy is also resistance. Thought is trying to escape into some future moment where it can be at peace instead of facing exactly what is arising now. For example, the moment you notice that there is a thought arising now that your wife should cook more often than she does, acceptance is happening. How could your wife cook more often than she does right now? That is impossible. Thought is arguing with reality. Thought is resistance. It is looking for some ideal future image of your wife rather than accepting who she is right now. Thought will not accept your wife. But awareness will. So when you are aware of your own thoughts of resistance to who your wife is in this moment, that is acceptance.

After the thought arises that she should cook more often, a second thought may arise that tells you that you need to be more accepting of your wife. Simply notice that thought too. That noticing is acceptance. How could you be other than who you are in this moment? That too is impossible. When you are trying to become more of anything, you are reaching for future, which is a dream of thought, and therefore you are avoiding what is in this moment, the only place where acceptance could ever happen. Do you see that true acceptance happens only now when resistance, analysis, and attachment to judgment stop? Analysis does not stop through more analysis. Judgment does not stop through more judgment. This all stops when you see it for what it is—the insanity of self. Do you see that thought is time? Do you see that thought is judgment, resistance, and analysis? Do you see that thought therefore cannot accept anything now because it is a dream of time? Only awareness of thought accepts. Stop and allow awareness to face directly your entire resistance to what is happening in this moment as well as your entire dream of becoming. That is true acceptance.

If you do not notice these mental strategies involved in the insanity of becoming, you stay stuck in the spiritual search, which means you keep self-centeredness alive. Any attempt to escape the reality of what is, is resistance to what is. That includes following some mind-made dream that some future moment will bring about acceptance of yourself or others. How could acceptance ever happen outside of this moment? When you place acceptance in time you make it into yet another carrot out beyond your reach. This is why it often feels as though you never quite fully accept yourself and others. I am not suggesting that you not ask your wife to cook more often. I am simply asking whether you feel the difference between the self-centered energy inherent in attachment to thoughts that resist what is and the more loving, surrendered energy present when you are noticing that resistance.

Effort will not bring acceptance because effort implies time, a movement to become or to escape what is arising now. Effort therefore is resistance to what is. True acceptance is the gentle, loving, and compassionate noticing of what is arising now in the mind and body and all around you. It is effortless. If you are applying effort to accept a situation, you are actually applying more resistance to it—more thought. Acceptance is being fully present with whatever is arising, including effort, resistance, or thoughts of becoming more accepting. Just notice. Gentleness, love, and compassion will take over from there. When action is taken from the surrendered, loving energy of presence, the entire world is transformed. Maybe then your wife will begin cooking more often for you—or maybe not. Either way will be fine.

Acceptance Happens Only in Your Absence

If there is a sense in this moment that you are more accepting than you were yesterday or three years ago, watch the mind make a self out of that. It is attaching to yet another story. You are not actually more accepting. Acceptance is not a game of accumulation. The ego loves the idea of winning points in its spiritual journey. There is no separate self to accept anything. When it feels as if you are more accepting, this simply means that consciousness is less entangled in the thought and emotion arising now. It has nothing to do with time, or more, or becoming, or self. The dream self is resistance to what is. You cannot take credit for acceptance because it happens only in the absence of you, the dream self, which means the absence of resistance to what is. When there is acceptance, thought and resistance are simply releasing their hold, which allows a deepening into the awareness of the present moment. So rather than becoming more accepting over time, you are simply experiencing the release of resistance now. You are experiencing the release of the dream of self, which is the cause of suffering.

Why is this distinction critical? Well, thought can easily strengthen the illusory separate self by comparing a previous moment of struggle to a present moment of release. This strengthens the dream self and the spiritual search, as you start to really believe that "you" are "coming to accept" yourself and life more over time. You falsely believe that you are creating acceptance. This becomes the new story to which you attach. It is how the spiritual ego is born and how the insanity of becoming continues. You are still the rat on the wheel. There are people in the world who gather together in spiritual communities, churches, Sanghas, twelve-step meetings, and other groups to convince themselves and each other that they are learning to accept more and that acceptance happens in time. There is nothing wrong with gathering together in spiritual communities. It can be healthy and life-affirming. But self-deception is unhealthy no matter whether it takes place in your head or in a discussion around a table.

If you believe you are an accepting person, you are telling yourself a story. There is nothing particularly good or bad about that story. But it is not ultimately true. Some situation will come along, sooner or later, to show you that the mental image of yourself as an "accepting person" or a "spiritual person" is not who you truly are. You may then beat yourself up mentally when the image of who you thought you were does not match the present life situation that is causing you to struggle. Instead of getting lost in stories of how you are spiritual or not spiritual, or accepting or not accepting, simply be with whatever is arising. That is true acceptance. Allow these false images and stories to deepen you into the real truth of who you are beyond all images and stories.

True acceptance comes from a spiritual power that has nothing to do with the dream self. One could say, it comes from God. It is the very nature of who we are under all of our struggles and strategies to accept and our claims or fears about our own spiritual progress towards acceptance. As Gangaji says, true acceptance is like a kiss from the divine, which gives you a glimpse of your true nature. You did not create it. You cannot take credit for it and remain in the truth. It happens only in the absence of your dream of self.

In complete acceptance of what is in this moment, the whole notion of looking for acceptance in the future does not arise. You do not even bother with the concept of "acceptance." Your whole future-based search for acceptance or self-acceptance is actually based in non-acceptance of what is in this moment. This is maddening, isn't it? Do you see it? Look. Your body is here, but your mind is there, in thoughts of future. When your mind is there, you do not notice what is here, which means you do not see that thought of future arising now. When you do not see that thought, it has the capacity to make you actually believe that something needs to happen in the future before acceptance can arise. That is an obvious lie.

You could spend a lifetime chasing this illusion called future acceptance of yourself, others, and life. In that chase, conflict inevitably arises between what is and what you think should be—between the reality of this moment and your constant search for the next moment. This conflict causes fear, anxiety, and stress in the body, which leads to illness and disease. Doctors have been trying to tell us this for years. Your spiritual search may be contributing to an early death. Don't make a problem out of that. Just notice the search whenever it arises. In that noticing, the search for future releases its hold on you and life in this moment is affirmed.

Ten
WAKING UP

Most people, even though they don't know it, are asleep. They're born asleep, they live asleep, they marry in their sleep, they breed children in their sleep, they die in their sleep without ever waking up. They never understand the loveliness and the beauty of this thing that we call human existence.

— *Anthony de Mello*

Waking up from the dream of separation is not a new religion. It is not a new belief system. It is that which sees all religions and belief systems. Is it not anything to learn. It is that which is aware of what is already occurring. Nothing needs to happen for awakeness to be realized. It is no different than simply opening your eyes to awaken from a dream at night. It is seeing the whole movement of the self and its entire dream that it is the center of life and separate from everything it sees. It is seeing in vivid detail the magnificent life all around you. Are you ready to wake up? More pointedly, are you ready to realize there is no one to wake up?

Pause between each paragraph below and breathe a few breaths. Allow the words to soak into your whole being and to point you to the aliveness within your body and all around you. Do not engage these words on the level of agreement and disagreement. Let beingness read these words.

As you are reading, notice any energy that leads you to think or feel that you should be getting something from these words. These words cannot give you what you already are. You are already whole. The most these words can do is remind you of this.

When you see these three marks [* * *] this is an invitation to stop reading, put the book down, and go about the business of life, taking these words with you as little pointers to the utter mystery of the present moment—a mystery that no words can truly touch.

Just notice.

Notice that you are living in a radiant mystery called life. And then notice that the words "radiant," "mystery," and "life" do not even come close to truly describing the brilliance and ordinariness of it. Notice that they are just thoughts pointing to an actuality all around you, and within you. Notice that you are not separate from that actuality.

Notice that life is a symphony of sights, sounds, smells, sensations, thoughts, feelings, states, and experiences. Notice that the beautiful music of this symphony can only be fully realized when there is no self pretending to be the conductor.

Notice how beautiful and big, and yet how empty, the space around you is when you go outside. It never ends. It embraces you.

Notice that this space is who you are. It is within you. It is you.

Notice that there are no problems until a thought reaches up to label something within your field of awareness as a "problem." "Problems" are perfectly designed to keep self-centeredness in place because you get to think about them, analyze them, and complain to yourself and others about them, including about how you are or are not overcoming them. This keeps the focus on you. Life is simply happening. It is not happening to you. It is happening whether you resist it or welcome it. You only think it is happening to you. This mode of thinking helps you keep the dream of a separate self alive.

Notice the self-centered nature of a thought, and notice the next thought that tells you that you should not be self-centered. It is all a dream of self-centeredness.

Notice the thought that tells you that you should be more present. That is impossible. In this moment, you cannot be anything other than what you already are, which is here in this moment. So if noisy thinking or non-presence is arising now, just notice that. That noticing is presence.

Notice when thought is arising, and when it is not. Notice that thought is not a problem. There is either thought or no thought. The only thing that would make thought a problem or would make either thinking or not thinking more important than the other is another thought. Just notice that thought too.

Notice that thought always comes from one of the three realms of self-centeredness (past, future, and resistance to now). Notice that when a thought arises, there is a sense of self invested in it. You often want to hold onto that thought, or analyze it with related thoughts, because all of it is telling some story about who you think you are. Even your thoughts about others are telling you who you are in relation to them. You cannot let go of thought. Only another thought would try something like that. Noticing these thoughts arise and fall is liberating. It allows them to let go of you.

* * *

Notice that, when your body feels a negative emotion, your mind is telling a story within one of the three realms of self-centeredness.

Notice that when thought reaches into future, a little anxiety or fear sometimes rises up in your body. This anxiety or fear is simply telling you that you have entered a dream which is not true. This dream is called "the separate you."

Notice that there is no such thing as a negative emotion until you label it that way. There is only energy arising within the body. Be completely with that energy. Do not avoid it or try to think it away. Do not escape what is.

Notice that, when conflict arises in an interaction with someone or in a given situation, you entered the interaction or situation with a preconceived thought that it would turn out a certain way. Conflict arises when your dreams about reality do not match reality. Thus, you brought conflict into the situation when you brought your dream into it. No one is the cause of your pain. You are simply dreaming that you have control. Rather than blaming people, situations, or even yourself, simply notice the content of your dream.

Notice that resentments towards others have nothing to do with them. You are simply believing a presently arising dream. In this dream, a person or situation was supposed to do what you wanted them to do. That is not reality. The source of your pain is never outside you. It results from your attachment to thought and emotion arising within you. Do not try to fix or overcome resentments. Just notice them. Feel them fully.

Notice that when someone is yelling at you, calling you names, or being offensive, no response is required. The pain felt by this self who is attacking you has nothing to do with you. In his dream, you are supposed to be the way he wants you to be. That is not reality. Just be the space in which that happens, and notice whatever emotional reaction arises within you. If you need to defend yourself, allow that defense to happen. Waking up is not about suppressing anything. It is about being aware of what is.

Notice that when you lie, you are often attempting to protect some illusory self-image. Once you see that there is no self to protect psychologically, most of the lies fade away on their own.

Notice the feeling of lack within when someone does not give you the praise, acknowledgment, or approval you are seeking. Realize that the problem has nothing to do with what they did or did not give you. The problem arose when you failed to feel directly this sense of lack in the moment it first appeared in your body. It then fueled painful and untrue thoughts about how others are responsible for your happiness and contentment. You are noticing that lack is an illusion.

* * *

Notice that each person, and each thing, is beautifully mysterious until the dream of judgment gets a hold of it.

Notice that judgment of others does not die just because someone or some book tells you that judgment is wrong, or because you believe God condemns it. It dies naturally when you realize that judgment of others is a method by which you define yourself through thought. Hidden within every outward judgment is an inward comparison. "He is fat (therefore I am not fat)" "She is an idiot (therefore I am smart)." When the self dissolves, the need to self-define dies with it. Judgment then quiets on its own.

Notice that you wish others would change or be the way you want them to be. That is not reality. That is your dream.

Notice that there is no way to truly cope with this larger concept called "addiction." The only sane way to deal with addictive behaviors is to notice whatever is arising now. If a craving or obsession arises, notice it without analyzing it. Let it arise within awareness. Do not tell stories about how you should not be experiencing what you are experiencing. Reality is whatever is arising. Do not argue with reality. That is insanity. Simply be aware of what is arising. Notice that all cravings and obsessions arise from a formless awareness within you, and dissolve back into it. Allow that formless awareness to become aware of itself. Once that awareness is aware of itself, you see that cravings and obsession simply arise less or not at all. And when they arise, you see that they are not the monsters you thought they were. They only have power when they remain unconscious.

In fact, they are insubstantial, temporary phantoms that have no power over you as long as they arise within full awareness.

Notice that there is no way to truly cope with this larger concept called "procrastination." It is a fiction. The only sane way to cope with procrastination is to notice whatever is arising now. If a thought arises that you do not want to clean the kitchen, notice the thought. It does not matter whether you clean the kitchen or not. Just notice the thought. And notice the secondary thought which attempts to beat you up mentally if you do not clean the kitchen. In noticing each one of these thoughts the moment they arise, the mind starts to quiet. A quiet mind is not telling itself to clean or not clean the kitchen. In that clarity, action is taken or not taken, without all the unnecessary analysis. A clear mind is more able to take clear, healthy action. Analysis simply postpones action and leaves you spinning in thought and self-centeredness.

Notice the thoughts that you tell yourself about being too fat, not attractive, not good enough, not smart enough, lazy, or irresponsible. These images have nothing to do with who you really are. They are past images which are weighing you down, and keeping you from taking clear, healthy action in this moment.

* * *

Notice your hand move to your plate while you are eating, and then up to your mouth. Feel the sensation of food being chewed and swallowed.

Notice the feeling of water rushing over your hands as you wash the dishes.

Notice your fingers moving as you type words onto your computer, and notice the space around the fingers.

Notice the beauty of an old, deteriorating building. It is simply dissolving into the mystery which gave birth to it.

Notice that when you listen to music with your whole being instead of just your ears or your mind, it feels as if it is emanating from deep within you. This is not limited to music. Realize that you are the instrument through which life is living itself.

Notice the way a book sits on a desk, and the way socks lie on the floor.

Notice the smile on your child's face, and the wag of your dog's tail.

Notice the smells all around you, whether it is the smell of flowers, a cake baking in the oven, or spoiled food in a trash can.

Notice the warmth in the air, a breeze blowing by, hitting your face and blowing through your hair.

Notice the cold wind. And notice that when you believe you are separate from that cold, it feels colder, but when you keep your attention in your inner body and are aware of the belief that you are separate from the cold, the wind seems to warm up.

Notice your attachment to outcomes. Notice that when you are showering in the morning, you are thinking of what you are going to do later that day. Notice that when you drive to work, you are thinking of what you need to do when you get there. Notice that when you get there, you are thinking that you would rather be somewhere else, wishing you were already done with the project you are working on, or wishing it were lunch or the end of the day. Notice that when the day is over, you sometimes still think about work.

Notice that when you start doing something, your mind is often on the end result, rather than the actual doing in each moment.

Notice that life is like a river rushing by and through you. It is constantly moving, yet there is a deeply silent, immovable awareness in you watching the whole thing. Thoughts, emotions, reactions, cars, books, dinners, pens, pets, jobs, words, relationships and all other forms are moving through this river. Notice that when your mind gets stuck on any particular form moving through the river, the dream self is trying to stop the river and gain control. Suffering arises because control is not possible. But notice that when the deeply silent, immovable awareness in you is simply watching this rushing river without getting stuck on any of the forms moving through it, it is like you are free-falling in space with nothing to hold onto and nowhere to land. That is liberation from the dream of self.

* * *

Notice that peace is absolutely here in this moment under all the energy of referencing the past and dreaming about the future.

Notice that your body is always here, but your thoughts are there, in some future or past dream. Do not make a judgment or belief out of that last sentence.

Don't point out to others that they are unconscious or not present. That is your dream about them. You are stuck in some past concept about them when you point outward in that way. Simply notice when thought is telling a story of past or future. That noticing automatically brings your attention to this moment where life truly is, beyond attachment to judgment and belief.

Notice that there is quietness under each sound, and that sound arises out of and falls back into that quietness.

Notice your breath coming in and out. Life is breathing you. How magnificently ordinary! You are alive, as life itself, and not in any way separate from it. You would not be alive if it were not for the air all around you.

Notice that when you start thinking about God, you enter a dream of thought and miss the beautiful manifestations of God right before your eyes.

Notice the feeling of irritation that arises when you are unable to fix the malfunctioning toaster. Then notice the space around that irritation. Notice that the broken toaster is not a problem until you make it a problem through thought.

Notice that when you are fully here in this moment a thought may arise that physical pain or discomfort should not be happening. That is not reality. Be with the pain or discomfort. Do not fight it. Notice the space around it, and within it. And then take an aspirin or go to the doctor if necessary.

Notice that when you look at a star with the thought in your head that you are a person looking at a star, the star seems very distant and separate. But when you look deeply with awareness, without the thought of yourself, the idea of you vanishes. There is only the seeing. And you and the star are one in a way the mind will never grasp as an idea.

Notice everything around you. Then notice how you label everything as chair, desk, furniture, room, building, street, and town. Notice that only thought separates reality into parts. In this moment, awareness is showing you that there are no separate things.

Notice the feel of the ground beneath your feet as you walk, and the clouds moving through the unchanging sky above.

* * *

Notice how others feel, what they say, what thoughts and emotions are arising within them. Notice the stark similarity between thoughts and feelings that others experience and those that you experience.

Notice the tone of your loved ones' voices, the depth in their eyes, and the sound of their breathing. Don't think about others. Your thoughts about them have nothing to do with them. They are your interpretations of what is.

Don't conclude that there is no one there in the other. Conclusions do not see. Just look, listen, and feel. Be the space for others.

Notice why it is that this moment never feels quite good enough, and why the mind keeps moving forward. Notice that you are not really moving forward. "Forward" is the dream.

Notice the insanity of becoming in each moment it manifests. Where are you going? Oh, even in presence, there is a sense of a self there, as well as a sense that life is unfolding in time. But if you look honestly, you realize that you do not know where that self begins or ends or what life is or if it has ever gone anywhere. Notice that the sense of moving through time as a separate self has been occurring in thought only. Life is always this moment. 'This."

Notice that when regret, shame, remorse, resentment, or anger is manifesting, you are telling a story that something which happened should not have happened. Is that true? How could it be? Whatever happened did in fact happen. That is the reality. The dream is that it should not have. That is your dream. Notice each thought within that dream, and how it is tied to maintaining this central idea of being a self completely separate from the rest of life. Everything you need to know about the past is surfacing in the moment these negative feelings arise. Feel each feeling the moment it arises.

In this noticing, the waking up happens on its own. Waking up is not a process. No time is needed, which means no mind is needed. But if thought arises, that is fine. Just look at what is already here in this moment no matter what it is. And then notice something even simpler, subtler, more obvious than anything noticed. Realize *that* which is noticing. There is a beingness that is prior to any thought, feeling, reaction, label, identity, resentment, or problem. Realize this beingness from within, and notice that every temporary thought or emotion you have ever experienced arose from it. You are not these temporary thoughts and emotions. You are this beingness. You are life itself. This beingness permeates everything you see from the street sign, to the ocean, to the thought arising now, to the baby crying in her cradle. When you are aware of the depth of this inward life, the depth of all life is being revealed to you. This is the True Self, beyond the ego. It is 'This.' Oneness. God.

This radiant mystery called life is being lived through you. Life is you, and you are life. No separation. Don't make a belief system or religion out of that. Just look.

In this noticing, you see life the way that it really is. Beautiful. Full. Fresh. New in each moment. You see it through the innocence of a child, with pure wonder—without the veil of the past. You see that life is extraordinary and sacred. Yet it is ordinary, simple, and unremarkable. It is doing the dishes, the clanking of plates hitting one another. It is reaching down to pick something off the floor, and then the noticing of every step to the trash can to throw it away. It is noticing the thought that you are noticing each step. Or it is noticing that you are not paying attention at all. It is the feel of bed sheets under your body as you lie down to sleep at night. Joy. It is noticing anger the moment it arises in your body. It is the sound of a dog barking and then licking herself. It is the kiss on your loved one's cheek. The sensation of skin. Love. It is putting in a DVD that ends up not working. Joy. It is sitting on the couch, hearing a car engine running outside, and noticing the deep silence from which that sound emanates. Peace. It is lungs breathing, papers shuffling, clocks ticking, children laughing, toes bending, head turning, and legs walking, and no one is there doing any of it. Do you notice this or are you too busy focusing on your illusory problems and thinking the dream self into existence?

Eleven
DO YOU SEE THE LOOP?

Only one koan matters—you.

— Ikkyu

The mind is a noisy, repetitive recording machine that plays the past over and over. When you say, "I can't wait to go to the movie on Thursday" or "I'm working towards becoming a better person," this is past conditioning. It looks like future, doesn't it? But how would your mind even know that going to a movie is an enjoyable or desirable thing if it had not learned that from a past experience of going to a movie or from a description given by someone else?

How would your mind be able to project a thought of what a future "better you" would look like if it did not already possess an image from something you learned in the past? Perhaps someone told you, or you learned in a self-help book, or through some past experience that a "good" person does this, and a "bad" person does that. So you memorize this image of good, and a thought arises in your mind that you must work towards matching who you are to this image of a good person. You call it spiritual progress when you are thinking thoughts of becoming this ideal in your own head or when your thoughts tell you that your actions are matching this ideal. In reality, this ideal is keeping you focused on you. This mechanism within you makes your entire thought realm self-centered. You, a thought, are only ever chasing a better version of you in the future, which is also thought. Thought is chasing itself. Do you see this?

This is what gives rise to the illusory spiritual search. So you are following some ideal or image that someone or something has imposed on you in the past. Perhaps it is an image of a spiritual person, religious person, or enlightened person. You are enslaved to some outside authority or to some image, which means you are enslaved to your own memory. You are deceiving yourself. You are not on a path to freedom in that case. You are not moving into the truth or into genuine spiritual transformation. You are only ever chasing your own conditioning. You are on a path to more self. Do you see the loop of self-centered thought? Thought is memory (past), coming to meet this moment, and projecting itself forward into a future dream where it seeks to confirm and strengthen what it already knows, which is memory (past). This entire mechanism keeps you in an illusion of becoming and that you are at the center of life.

True Goodness

What is truly good is totally outside of your conceptions of good v. bad. True goodness is love itself. It is outside of this loop you have created in which you are chasing your own thought. The truth is, you are only ever right here, right now, which is the perfect and only place from which to see this loop for what it is, and therefore to realize the good that is beyond the loop. There can only be good beyond the loop. The loop is self-centeredness.

I am not implying that you should suppress any of these thoughts or memories of good v. bad. Only thought would want to suppress itself. In that case, thought would be creating an image in the mind that an enlightened person does not think. It would then chase after that image—its own projection. You would still be within the loop.

I am simply asking whether you notice what is already here, a loop of self-centeredness. The past is continuously coming to strengthen what it already knows and to project itself into future. This is why victims often stay victims their whole lives. This is why arrogant people never seem to change. They are only ever consulting their own thought, which is the past, to tell them who they are, where they have been, and where they are going. They are stuck in the loop of ego. The ego is a well-oiled machine, perfectly designed to continue chasing after its own memory, which it projects forward as an illusion called "future." Nothing new arises in that loop.

When I say nothing new arises in that loop, I do not mean that you should place some new thought, idea, or spiritual method within the loop that will magically allow you to step out of that loop. No, that would just be creating another image to chase after. All thought is of the past. So no matter what thought you put there, it is not new. I am just asking: do you notice this in each moment? Are you looking at this loop of thought?

When something new is presented, the mind searches its database looking for the familiar. It says, "Oh yeah, this new thing is like the old thing I already know." It files the new thing away as "something known." It often disregards information that it has never stored into memory. It looks only for what it already recognizes, because it is only ever seeking to confirm the truth of the content of its own loop. But the real truth cannot be known through thought. The "truth" is just another name for who you really are, beyond this loop. These thoughts coming from this illusory thing we call "ego" or "the loop" cannot touch reality, or truth. Only awareness can. Only awareness will see the new. The content of the loop will only repeat itself. Awareness always sees the new because awareness is presence itself. The present moment is always new. The content of the loop is old and repetitive. Awareness sees the content of the loop arising now. In bringing awareness to that loop, insight arises. Insight is always revealing that there is no ego. Through presence, awareness also becomes aware of itself.

Within the movement of this loop, thought is looking for agreement and disagreement on the level of the mind. This agreement and disagreement strengthens the loop and its separateness from other loops. When a loop finds agreement, it strengthens what it already knows. This newfound agreement feeds memory, feeds thought, which then goes about seeking further strengthening, further confirmation of itself in future. Disagreement does the same thing, except that it provides an entirely different and necessary dimension. Disagreement allows a loop to compare and contrast itself against other loops. Opposition is the fuel here. Either way, the loop feeds and strengthens itself. Suffering comes from self-centeredness and separation. Self-centeredness and separation continue until you notice this loop operating.

Wisdom Sees the Loop

True spiritual insight is not repeating some spiritual saying you learned. You can believe "all thought is of the past" or anything else a spiritual teacher tells you. But until you see these things operating within you, no true insight comes. The repetition of spiritual ideas is only memory, no matter how fancy the saying. There is nothing wrong with spiritual ideas. But true insight is fresh and new. It is looking at what is arising right here and now in the mind. In that noticing, wisdom arises.

Wisdom is like a breath of fresh air. It is totally transformative. Wisdom does not mean that you will not enjoy the movie on Thursday. It means you will be aware of the movie playing in your own head right now about the movie on Thursday. It does not mean that good will not be realized. Wisdom shows you that "good" is what you truly and naturally are beyond all your stories of "good" vs. "bad."

Wisdom is intelligent presence. Presence naturally dissolves the self-centered loop created from childhood or from your unsatisfactory past. This presence allows you to finally see life the way that it really is. You are no longer experiencing this moment through the dead repetition of the past. If a spiritual insight is realized by wisdom in this moment, that insight cannot be carried forward in time. If it is carried forward and made into a belief, it becomes part of the loop of self. It becomes spiritual knowledge, which is fuel for the spiritual ego.

A spiritual ego believes that it knows something and that this knowledge makes it more spiritual than others. Therefore, it has trapped itself back into the loop of self-centeredness and separation. Wisdom sees. It does not make a self out of what is seen.

Twelve
WISDOM VS. KNOWLEDGE

Don't seek the truth. Just cease to cherish opinions.
— *Zen saying*

*Stop looking from your cloud of hazy thoughts. Looking
from that vantage point is pure folly. Look from behind that
cloud of thinking. There it is always clear.*
— *Adyashanti.*

The notion of "consciousness waking up from the
dream of thought" is itself a dream phrase. It is a story
about what is. It is not ultimately true that consciousness
"wakes up." It is already awake. Nonetheless, the phrase
is one way of pointing to this truth called enlightenment.

Knowledge

I use the distinction between knowledge and wisdom
as another way to point to this spiritual awakening. In the
mind-identified or egoic dream state, a person believes
that she is a separate self, and that everything that she
thinks about reality is in fact true. This is the nature of
attachment or identification with thought. Within the
dream, her thoughts, interpretations, and beliefs tell her
who she thinks she is, in relation to the others, which are
also just thoughts in her dream. In this thought realm,
she is the ruler of the kingdom. She believes that her
religion, her belief system, her thoughts about others
and the world, her opinions, and her interpretations are

correct. In order to maintain that illusion, she must make others wrong. She may not always share this out loud or realize it, but thought is telling this story nonetheless. "Unconsciousness" simply means to "not see" that this is occurring.

So when she labels this as a "table," thinks her husband "ought to not talk so much," opines that "Christianity is foolish," or whatever the case may be, she falsely believes that these thoughts objectively explain what is happening "out there" in the world that she sees. She does not see that thought is essentially just memory—subjective conditioning. It is a conceptual overlay placed by the mind over the reality of what is. This overlay keeps the illusion of separateness and therefore self-centeredness alive. After all, without her interpretations, without her story (including her complaints, labeling, arguments, blaming, disagreeing, and opinions), who would she be in relation to what she sees? There would be no separate self there, which means there would be only reality.

This overlay constitutes her "knowledge." Knowledge is a set of files stored away as memory. It is past conditioning that comes to meet what she sees in the present moment and to project itself forward into future. This is the ego strengthening and maintaining itself and its future survival. This knowledge can be very helpful. It has such important practical applications. It has been necessary to the survival of the human species, letting us know when to take shelter from a storm, or how to find food. It is important in the advancement of technology, medicine, and law. But when knowledge becomes hijacked by the psychological ego, it causes suffering. It engages in a game of separating itself from illusory others through agreement and disagreement. Knowledge, when hijacked by ego, becomes a weapon of separation. This is why a person feels "attacked" and gets defensive when someone challenges her belief system or criticizes her thoughts or actions.

Fear is the glue of the ego. It holds it together. The ego is afraid of vulnerability and sensitivity. It is afraid of being wrong. It is literally afraid to love openly. Ultimately, it is afraid of death, which it sees as the end of itself. This is why true intimacy is often difficult. True intimacy devours the ego. The ego is very fragile and self-protective. After all, it is an illusion that must go to great lengths (constant thinking) to keep itself in place and to protect itself from the other illusions, which it perceives as threats to its continued separateness. The ego is in a tug of war between loving and fearing others. Ego, as the psychological realm of knowledge, is a mechanism of self-protection.

Wisdom

Wisdom is something else entirely. It is a quiet mind which sees reality the way it is. It is an honest, inward looking at this psychological realm. Without inward honesty and sincerity, the self stays within its dream of self-centeredness. Wisdom is that which sees the whole dream operating in each moment. It is that which sees the knowledge being pointed outward to defend and protect the self from feeling fear directly and from loving openly. Wisdom sees that you are far more than a mechanism of self-protection. You are life itself.

Knowledge cannot see this. It can merely point to it and think about it.

Wisdom is the eye of God within us. Wisdom is completely aware of knowledge. Knowledge knows nothing of wisdom. Knowledge can only think and play old files. Wisdom sees not only what is being thought, but also that there is no separate self beyond these files. There is no self at the center of life despite what thoughts are saying. Nothing in this book should be construed as a suggestion to suppress self. This book is merely asking whether you notice the story it is telling.

Wisdom realizes that the entire interpretation (knowledge) is a conceptual overlay. It sees the conceptual overlay being projected outward from the thoughts of others. It realizes all of this is a dream, and that seeing is much deeper, and more loving and compassionate than anything the dream can conjure up.

Wisdom is realized only through the discerning eye of presence. It stares directly into the face of resistance and separation. In this way, it is vulnerable, sensitive, and loving. This is what frees a person from the notion that he is a self, separate from the rest of life. It also frees him from his fear of death. From the dream state, it may appear that this wisdom that is always noticing what is arising within is just more self-centeredness. But that is just the mind's way of keeping thought as the ruler of the kingdom, so it does not have to really look at what is here and to really face fear. In reality, wisdom is the way out of self-centeredness. The phrase "consciousness waking up from the dream of thought" is just another way of saying "wisdom becoming aware of knowledge."

Do not suppress anything, least of all knowledge. Let knowledge arise and fall as it will. Wisdom notices knowledge pointing outward into the dream of its own creation. Knowledge only ever sees its own dream. Wisdom sees beyond the dream into the truth of what is.

Thirteen
OUTWARD POINTING INTO YOUR OWN DREAM

As a man is, so he sees.

— *William Blake*

*Thinking that people are supposed to do or be anything other
than what they are is like saying that the tree over there
should be the sky. I investigated that and found freedom.*

— *Byron Katie*

There is an old saying, "The world is a reflection of
your own mind." J. Krishnamurti used to say, "You are the
world and the world is you." These are pointers to reality
itself, beyond the interpretation of the ego and its illusion
of separation. Your thoughts simply make up your own
conceptual overlay, your interpretation of reality. They are
not objectively true. They constitute your dream.

When you judge others, you are only pointing
outward into your own dream of thought, your own
conceptualization of how things should have been,
how they should be now, and how they should be in
the future. Your judgments towards others tend to
speed up or happen more frequently when there is fear
or insecurity within you. This is simply the fragile ego
trying to protect itself by diminishing the value of the
other illusory egos. Your entire realm of judgments
about yourself and others is a mental dream. This is why
judgment causes such harm. It is not based in truth.

Everyone believes he or she is right. That is what identification with thought is. Yet, not everyone can be right, objectively speaking. "Right" is only what you believe it is. Your ideas of "right" and "good" are self-serving concepts that are obscuring the natural goodness within.

Do you see what is happening in relationships? We mistake our thoughts, our opinions, and our beliefs for the truth, and look for agreement and disagreement through others, all in an effort to strengthen our interpretation of reality—to confirm what we already know. This is the nature of self-centeredness.

This does not mean that you should not speak your mind. Thoughts, opinions, and beliefs belong to the world of form. You can express these things, and play with them. But there is a formless awareness within you that sees that you are only sharing the details of your particular conceptual overlay. Awareness then becomes aware of itself. That awareness is not mistaken. It sees that thought is self-centered. It sees that thought is essentially memory, projecting itself (pointing itself outward to the world) to confirm what it already knows, so that it can strengthen itself and its separation from the others.

There is no such thing as stepping out of the dream, right? We cannot annihilate thought through personal will. That would be applying resistance to resistance. In fact, we do not want to suppress anything. The only thing that would want to suppress thought is another thought. Awareness is the key to spiritual transformation. But awareness happens only now. It does not happen in time or through personal will. Awareness is already aware in this moment, all you have to do is notice that.

Spiritual awakening involves the pure clarity of seeing that, when thought points outward to the "other" to say, "This should not be as it is," or "That shouldn't have happened," the dream is dreaming itself. You are simply expressing the details of your own conditioning. Your thoughts are not objectively true. Until this is realized, life will continue to be a struggle on one level or another. Until you see that you are creating the dream (through mental interpretation of what is) and then attempting to argue with your own creation (outward pointing into your own interpretation), self-centeredness stays in place. It is a closed-circuit system, perfectly designed to create internal suffering. Suffering is there to teach you that you are lost within an illusion of separation and self-centeredness.

The dream of separateness and self-centeredness also includes what psychologists sometimes call the shadow or disowned self. When you see a quality in another person that you despise or judge harshly, it is often because you are seeing a shadow of yourself in that person. In other words, if you find yourself fixating on the story of how someone is controlling or manipulative, it is often because you have repressed those same qualities in yourself. You have pushed them away. They become shadows of your ego, projected outward onto others. It is not enough just to be aware of these judgments or stories as they arise. You must own them and realize that your judgments of others have nothing to do with them. It may be that the person you are judging is actually controlling or manipulative. But why does that bother you so much? As these judgments arise, see whether there are controlling or manipulative qualities within yourself that you have repressed and projected onto the other through outward judgment. If so, turn that outward judgment inward. Make it a story of self because that is what it is, except that it has been repressed and projected outward. If you find it difficult to own it, say to yourself, "I am controlling" and "I am manipulative." Tell the truth. You cannot transcend the shadow self until you own it and realize that it has nothing to do with the other. Once you own the story, you can transcend it by being fully aware of it as a story of ego and by feeling directly whatever feelings arise when you own it.

Notice what is happening when you believe others are judging you. Even before others open their mouths, you may feel a sense of paranoia as you sense that they are judging you negatively. These judgments are often your own egoic projections. Relationship is a mirror in that regard. Others are merely acting as a mirror, reflecting back to you those attributes in yourself that you have repressed. If you feel that others are judging you, for example, as fat, ignorant, not spiritual, poor, or unintelligent, this is often a repressed story of self being reflected back to you. Your own mind is creating judgment from others even where there is no actual judgment coming from others. Until you see this as a story of self, rather than judgment from others, the story cannot be transcended and no clear action to improve a situation can take place. When others do open their mouths to judge you negatively, watch what happens:

if a person's judgment about you is just plain wrong, you will feel very little need to defend yourself. But if her judgment matches some negative self-image that is repressed within you, you will defend yourself and possibly attack her back. This defense and attack energy is telling you that, on some level, you believe the negative judgment is true. Until you realize that relationship is a mirror and is constantly revealing your story of self, true spiritual awakening cannot happen. True spiritual awakening is realized when the entire movement of self is owned and transcended through pure awareness. Action can then be taken from awakeness, not from a repressed or projected (unconscious) story of self.

This spiritual awakening allows for a whole new way of being in the world. This beingness is unconditional love itself. This does not mean you will not have thoughts, opinions, and beliefs anymore. You may. Or you may not. And you may or may not share them, or point outward. Only another thought would care about any of that. This beingness is THAT which is aware of all these thoughts. It is the essence of who we are beyond the dream. Everything you see, touch, think, feel, taste, hear, and smell arises within this essence. It arises within love.

The ego will never realize unconditional love because it is essentially a set of conditions. You, as a thought-based entity, are imposing those conditions on external circumstances and projecting the story of self outward. You are the world and the world is you. Instead of thinking about whether unconditional love is possible, which is purely philosophical masturbation, simply notice in each moment each condition you place on people and situations. Notice when you are pointing outward into your own dream. These conditions can only continue in the dark. As each condition comes up into the light of awareness, it fades away on its own. Once the set of conditions fades, the dream self fades. Unconditional love is what is left when the dream of self dissolves.

Only this inward looking will see that outward pointing is false. This looking frees you from the loop of self-centeredness, so that you see yourself for who you really are, not who you think you are. It frees you to see that others are not who you think they are either. This is when relationships get out of the mind, and into the heart, so to speak. Enlightenment could be summed up as, "When love begins seeing itself everywhere as itself." Love destroys the illusory boundary between inward and outward, between self and other.

The Holy War Within

. . . methods have divided man; you have your method, and somebody else has his method, and these methods are everlastingly quarrelling with each other.

– J. Krishnamurti

You may preach non-violence for the rest of your life and all the time be sowing the seeds of violence.

– J. Krishnamurti

Fourteen
IS SPIRITUAL INSIGHT YOURS?

*Truth or Reality cannot be stored, cannot be amassed—
it does not accumulate. The value of any insight,
understanding, or realisation can only be in the ever-fresh
presence of the moment.*

— 'Sailor' Bob Adamson.

An insight is an "aha" moment where something
becomes very clear spiritually. The truth that is recognized
in a genuine insight is often unrecognizable. It is not
simply the recognition of some memory or knowledge
within the mind, or the result of learning from a spiritual
book, teacher, or tradition. Although a book, teacher, or
tradition may point you in the direction of the truth, a
true insight is something entirely different than belief, or
the recognition in one's own mind of something learned
or memorized.

This is what makes it an "aha" moment. The truth
shocks you. It comes from outside the psychological
loop (or tape recording) of your conditioning. One
could say, it comes from God. But to say with any sense
of mental certainty that it comes from God or from
enlightenment or self-realization is to strip the "aha"
away from it, bringing it into the known, and making
it into something learned or memorized. Insight gets
killed by memory. Every spiritual teacher and spiritual
book, including this one, must step into the dream of

thought—into past insights, memory—to point to the truth, which is now.

True insight happens only in this moment. It is new and fresh. It cannot be carried forward over time. Time is simply mind. So carrying it forward just means making it into memory. Memory, if you identify with it, becomes ego. True insight opens up the mind to what is. Insight is not thought. Insight is the act of seeing into the nature of something. It is that which sees thought. It allows you to see the ego for what it is—a dream of separation. Insight does not confirm what the mind already knows, except as a matter of coincidence. It takes you out of self, rather than confirming what you already know or who you think you are. The seeking of confirmation of what one already knows is memory, conditioning, past, or belief searching only to recognize and strengthen itself. This seeking is the spiritual search itself.

The mind looks for appearances in reality for which it can essentially say, "Yes, this confirms what I already know." The mind is looking for security and certainty in that sense, not realizing that it is only getting more of the same conditioning. It is not looking for truth. It has fooled itself into believing that it already knows. And so what it finds is only itself. Ultimately, this seeking of confirmation is ego. But this ego is shaky and fragile because it must always seek to defend and confirm itself as "right," so there is ultimately no security or certainty in it.

Memory, belief, and knowledge are not new and fresh. When a memory of a past spiritual insight comes back around, the mind, if it is not alert, falsely believes that it is having an insight, not realizing it is merely seeing its own mental projection. True insight does not come from thought. It comes from awareness, which is that which sees thought. Thought merely conceptualizes what is seen. This conceptualization is useful. After all, this book could not have been written without it. But insight itself is a moment by moment looking at what is arising.

Spiritual insight is not yours. It does not belong to the "me." The ego cannot gain anything from it. You do not get to be a better version of yourself through spiritual insight. True spiritual insight allows you to see through this self that is creating conflict, suffering, and division on earth. Look at the wars, politics, religious disagreement, terrorism—all of it. Belief systems are fighting and separating themselves from other belief systems. These divisions and conflicts have nothing to do with the truth. Thought is simply bumping into thought. One self is defending his interpretation of the truth at the expense of the other. Man has become more interested in defending his own path, method, tradition, group, country, religion and belief system than in openness, love, and discovering what is absolutely true.

Once you carry insight with you, accumulating it over time, you make belief systems out of it. On the one extreme end, you fly planes into big buildings and blow yourself up in crowds. But at the other end, you have a "gentleman's debate" about God outside of church, or about the nature of 'This' in an online non-duality chat room. Is God debating? Does God debate? Does 'This' argue with itself? Who is debating whom?

One self (one set of memories and conditioning) is debating another self (another set of memories and conditioning). You cannot take true refuge by merely pointing to the terrorist's belief system as "much worse" or "more delusional." This, in and of itself, is an attempt to strengthen your own egoic belief system. It's a classic example of "I am right and you are wrong." It is just more separation. Belief is the real weapon of mass destruction.

For true spiritual insight to occur, you must look at this whole movement of self, the ways in which the conditioning is separating you from your fellow man, your religion from other religions, your church from other churches, your country from other countries. This is why the realization that it is all One devours the sense of separate self. It sees the truth, which is that the self is a dream, built on conflict and separation. This separation is happening at all levels—nation against nation, church against church, belief against belief, spouse against spouse. The human mind has fragmented into millions of divisions. It is pure madness. In the realization of Oneness, all division is devoured. Everything that is not true is swallowed up.

If anything, insight shows you what you do not know. This is why it is so disarming, so loving. When insight comes, it is not smug. You do not get to be someone in relation to someone else. You are not higher than or better than anyone else for insight that arises within you. True insight is humility itself, which devours you as a separate person. If an insight moves you, it moves you for the benefit of the whole, for love itself, not for your own personal benefit or to have your story of spiritual truth or your religion confirmed.

What is left after true realization is not a new belief system, church, synagogue, religion or tradition. It is love itself. Love is not a thought or a belief system. It exists outside of thought. It is always here, now. It is not part of the psychological loop of self. As the self and its dream of time dissolve, love is realized as the natural state of humanity. Love reveals that separation is a mental illusion. True insight opens awareness up to the realization that all is One.

Fifteen
LOSING YOUR RELIGION

When they lose their sense of awe, people turn to religion.
— *Lao-tzu, Tao Te Ching*[3]

You are going to remain a Hindu, a Parsi, a Buddhist, a follower of some guru. That way you maintain division; therefore you maintain conflict. Where there is conflict, there must be pain, suffering, and in that there is no love.
— *J. Krishnamurti*

This inquiry is not intended to encourage you to give up your religion or to stop going to church, synagogue, or mosque. It is an inquiry that, if you take inward, will waken you from the conceptual dream of religion and allow you to deepen into the present moment, where the true depth, reality and presence of God and religion rests—and to see that depth everywhere including in other religions.

The phrase "losing my religion" is an expression from the southern region of the U.S., and means losing one's peace, or "flying off the handle." Apparently, the underlying notion is that religion brings peace or is peace.

Religion and the False Sense of Certainty and Security

What is religion to the conceptual mind? It is a belief or set of beliefs, yes?

Does one find true peace through a set of beliefs? Or is true peace something else entirely? Do not seek to answer that with some conclusion, which may lead to another religion. Look with me.

A belief is a thought that is not absolutely true or that you do not know to be absolutely true, right? If it were absolutely true, without a doubt, and supported by unquestionable direct proof, you would not use the word "belief." You would call it absolute truth or truth. Of course, the line may become blurry in your mind. You may strongly want something to be true. So your conviction, your hope, your desire to know pulls you into believing that a thought is true, even in the absence of direct proof.

But why do you do this? Why do you blur the line? Are you seeking a sense of certainty, security, and peace? Is this seeking emanating from this conviction, hope, and desire to believe? Is it emanating from an inner lack of certainty, security, and peace? Is this not a spiritual search? For what are you searching? Do not place more conclusions, more beliefs, on these questions. Just look. Notice.

If you find yourself defending your beliefs, or insisting that others' beliefs are wrong, you have found neither certainty, security, nor peace. Instead, you have found conflict. Only what is absolutely true will bring peace, yes? Anything less than that will become a belief, which you will have to defend in order to keep your false sense of security and certainty. If spirituality does not seek to answer the question "what is absolutely true," then it is nothing more than an escape into fairytale land. It is ego.

The Self-Centered Nature of Thought

Why are you unhappy? Because 99.9 percent of everything you think, and of everything you do, is for yourself. And there isn't one.

— *Wei Wu Wei*

In order to see what is true, you must see what is false. If you are seeking a sense of certainty, why seek it in thought? Thought is a fragment. It cannot see the whole of life. It is only interested in itself. When you think something is true, something that you do not know to be absolutely true, you are that thought, are you not? You are identified with that thought, and totally lost within it. There is a sense of self in that thought. Are you already disagreeing with me? Where does your disagreement come from? It comes from a sense of self which you have invested in your own thoughts. There is no peace in this investment. This investment is too busy defending and attacking, agreeing and disagreeing.

Thought measures, compares, insists, demands, wants, seeks, debates, argues, agrees, disagrees, describes, and defines. These movements tell you who you think you are in relation to the other. You, as a thought-based entity, are very complicated. The more you think about a situation, the more complex the process of thought becomes. It is like a cancer, constantly proliferating. There is no peace in the noise of this constant thinking. You may find agreement or disagreement through thought, which may confirm the thought-based self, but you will not find what is absolutely true through thought. Therefore, you will not realize peace.

If you stumble upon some fancy belief, or thought, or saying, and you believe it is the absolute truth, watch what happens when that is challenged. What happens when someone challenges your thoughts? You feel unsteady, defensive. What are you defending? Are you defending the truth? Surely not. You are defending the sense of self that is tied into your thoughts.

Self-centeredness is purely a product of thought. When you have a thought of yourself, you are only interested in that thought. You are only interested in the self. In that way, you separate yourself from the rest of life. You are doing it. It is not objectively true that you are separate. Subjectively, through your own thought process, you create an illusion of separateness between you and your fellow man, your beliefs and others' beliefs. You make yourself right by making the other wrong. This is spiritual violence.

Look at each one of your thoughts. Is not the majority of thought self-centered, unless it is simply reporting on what is being observed, or inquiring into the nature of something? You may say, "Not all thought is self-centered. I don't always think about myself." Take a look at even that response. Whom are you defending? You are defending a thought-based self that is claiming not to be self-centered. In that defense, you have placed yourself at the center once again. You have placed thought at the center as the defender of itself. This thought-based self is essentially obsessed with itself. It is always defending itself, thinking about itself, talking about itself, comparing itself to others, claiming that it has or has not found God, that it exists or does not exist or that it "does not always think about itself."

Even when you think about something that is seemingly unrelated to the self, is not that thought often self-centered also? You have labeled and categorized everything around you. Through endless naming and categorizing, you have divided this One Life into many, many fragments. You place a corresponding value on each fragment depending on what it can give you, how it relates to you, or what you like and dislike about it. I am not asking you to stop using names and labels or to suppress your likes and dislikes. That would be impossible and silly. Enjoy the whole play of naming, labeling, liking, and disliking. I am not trying to convince you to believe that all thought is self-centered. That would just create another religion by which you could separate yourself from the others who do not see it. I am inviting you to see for yourself. See that, according to thought, everything is yours: your experiences, your friends, your job, your car, your partner, your life, your country, and your religion. All of that is a dream. Outside of thought, you own and possess nothing. I am simply asking, "Do you see how thought keeps alive the dream that self is at the center of life?"

You can go on thinking that you know what things are. You can walk down the road and think that you know that this is a house, that is a road, this is a fence, and that is a mailman. Look more closely, is any of that absolutely true? Is that what this is? This is a mailman? That is a road? These could have been called a "jugnu" and a "hugit," just the same, right? Our naming of these things has nothing to do with their true essence.

Once you believe something to be true or place thought upon what you see, you do not have to look anymore, do you? Awareness shuts down, or is obscured by the placement of that thought. You have done this to everything in the world. Now you live within a conceptual overlay—a thought-based dream in which you are the center. You cannot see the beauty and Oneness which is actually here in life. You cover and divide it up with thought. There is no blame in any of this. Innocence has simply been replaced by self-centeredness. I am not proposing a new belief system in which there is a division between those who see Oneness and those who do not. That would just be more madness. I am only inviting you to see for yourself that the difference between thought and reality is startling. Beyond thought, there is no self.

Escaping Reality into Belief Systems

Why do you escape into belief systems? You believe because you are seeking certainty, yes? You believe that thought will provide this certainty. But isn't there uncertainty and fear under this seeking? Of course there is. Don't agree or disagree. Agreement and disagreement is just more belief. Look at what is arising within you in the moment you cling to belief. For example, the belief that "tomorrow will be better" has at its core this underlying fear that tomorrow will not be better. In fact, the whole notion of tomorrow being better would not arise if it were not for dissatisfaction, uncertainty, fear and lack arising today. Go directly into the dissatisfaction, uncertainty, fear and lack that underlie these beliefs. Look at the ways in which you are desperately trying to cover up these things and pretend that they are not here. You are escaping reality, are you not? You are escaping into fairytale land. You are telling stories about tomorrow, instead of facing what is arising now.

Fully facing these things frees you from them. Are you willing to lose your conceptual religion entirely and face reality directly? Your conceptual religion is not bringing peace. It is bringing confusion, conflict, and separation, and it is strengthening self-centeredness.

When I use the term religion, I am in no way limiting that to beliefs about God. Let's say that you woke up this morning, and your car did not start. Did you lose your peace, and "fly off the handle"? Or maybe your reaction was more subtle—a curse word or two, and a minor feeling of frustration. If you look closely, you will see that you had an unconscious belief operating before you turned the key of your car. Your religion before you turned the key was, "My car should start," or "Cars should generally start." Is that absolutely true? In reality, cars do not always start. Sometimes they do. Sometimes they do not. That is reality. In fairytale land, people tell stories that cars should always start. This religion causes confusion and frustration the moment a car does not start. Are you willing to lose this religion? Don't try to lose it. Noticing it allows it to fall away.

The term "religion" is often associated with a central deity or God. But in fairytale land, the ego is God. The ego is central. It has an elaborate set of beliefs that keeps it in place as the ruler of the kingdom. So you go to church on Sunday or perhaps to a synagogue, mosque or some other place of worship where the centrality of God is discussed. You hear about God as the supreme being who knows and controls everything. You praise God with your belief. You tell your friends and yourself that this God is in control. Then you leave your place of worship and drive down the road. When the guy in the car ahead of you is not driving fast enough, what happens? Do you lose your peace again? Your religion is apparently that people should drive the speed limit or should drive at the speed you prefer. Is it absolutely true? Who is playing God? Who is the central deity now? You are. This is why thought is self-centered. It keeps the self at the center. As you complain about the guy in the car ahead of you, you get to feel "right" or "better than." All of your complaints are fueling your sense of a separate self. If you look more closely, that guy is showing you where your religion is. He is your spiritual teacher. He is teaching you that your religion is not bringing peace. It is merely keeping the sense of a separate self in place.

When your dog barks loudly, or your husband does not listen to you in the way you would like, or your boss does not give you the acknowledgment that you think you deserve, look at the unconscious beliefs operating underneath your reactions. Are you arguing with reality? Are you covering up reality with an elaborate set of thoughts that place you at the center? Do you believe something should be happening other than what is happening? Then that is your religion. The reality is that you have no control and that you do not know. In fairytale land, you believe you are in control and that you know.

The True Peace of God

> *Thou canst understand nought about God, for He is above*
> *all understanding. A master saith: If I had a God whom*
> *I could understand, I would never hold Him to be God.*
> — *Meister Eckhart*

Are you finding peace in fairytale land? Is your religion bringing you peace? I have no argument with the religions of the world, such as Christianity, Hinduism, or Islam. There is a deep truth in all of them. As Eckhart Tolle has expressed, a belief in God is a "poor substitute" for the living reality of God manifesting in each moment. Are you at one with the living reality (God) or are you living in a dream that reality should be something different than what it is (fairytale land)?

God cannot be known through thought. The major religions are based on this deeper truth of not knowing, not resisting, and not trying to control. The word Islam, for example, means "submission" or the total surrender of oneself to God. This is pointing to the absence of the thought-based self and therefore the realization that only God is. Instead of seeing this truth that is beyond belief, will you simply continue in your belief in a God who is in control? Belief gives the dream self the illusion of control and knowledge and keeps it at the center of life, does it not? Is this not what beliefs do? You believe your religion is the truth and that other religions are false. Belief necessarily separates and fragments reality. A Christian must believe that Islam is false in order to sustain his belief that Christianity is true, and vice versa. That is the dream of separation. Man has become more interested in proving his own belief system, than in knowing the truth to which the word God points.

You, the ego, are therefore responsible for every holy or other war. It is not the fault of some politician, religion, or nation somewhere "out there" in the world. War is a manifestation of mind. Every time you insist on the supremacy of your belief system, you set in motion a ripple of spiritual violence. The mind is projecting its fragmentation, its violent divisive belief systems, out into the world. When it sees an enemy, it is seeing the details of its own egoic dream. Peace can only be realized when this war-making machine called thought is brought into the light of awareness in this moment.

The Bible states:

> *Being asked by the Pharisees when the kingdom of God would come, Jesus answered them, "The kingdom of God is not coming with signs to be observed, nor will they say, 'Look, here it is!' or 'There!' for behold, the kingdom of God is in the midst of you."* [4]

It is in the midst of you. It is now, in the present reality of what is. It is not in an escape from reality into the dream of time, which is the dream of self. It is not in divisive beliefs, concepts, signs, symbols, ideas or thoughts, all of which can merely point to it. In Romans 12:2, Paul said, "[d]o not conform any longer to the pattern of this world, but be transformed by the renewing of your mind." [5] Renew means to make new, fresh in each moment. Pattern is past. Belief is a pattern of thought coming from memory. It is not new or fresh.

It is old, stale, rigid, and inflexible. Belief cannot see what is here now because it is memory. Renewal happens when awareness wakes up to the reality of now, to the innocence and true intelligence of this moment.

In the total surrender of presence, you allow the living reality of God to manifest through you. You stop trying to know, control, and resist. When the self, as a separate thought-based entity, is surrendered completely, it vanishes. When the self vanishes, God is given his rightful place as the "living reality." This literally means living in reality—in the full acceptance of what is.

What will see "the peace of God, which surpasses all understanding . . . " mentioned in the Bible? It will not be mental certainty, right? Is there such a thing? Doubt and fear underlie all mental certainty. So belief creates a personal sense of false security and certainty. It separates and creates conflict. Belief cannot see the whole. It is only interested in sustaining itself. Belief is at odds with all other beliefs that in any way contradict it. It is therefore at odds with the whole. Religion itself is not a problem. It is a beautiful manifestation of 'This.' It can be a great vehicle to the truth. For some, it may even be a necessary vehicle for the realization of the true peace of God. But when religion is hijacked by the ego, it causes suffering, division, and conflict.

The mind cannot know peace through belief. Thought is movement, not rest. Thought, in and of itself, creates no problem. But when thought is not watched, not noticed, we are identifying with it. We believe virtually every bit of it. It is constantly moving, trying to escape and argue with reality and with others. Peace is realized by watching, noticing how the mind resists what is, how it separates, how it argues with reality, and how it operates on unconscious beliefs.

When the mind is clear, at rest, living at one with what is, there is peace. True peace is literally beyond belief. Are you ready to transcend the concept of religion and know the true depth and peace of God to which that concept is pointing—a depth and peace that is beyond thought and belief? This depth transcends religion, but also includes and celebrates it. If you are ready, start looking at thought rather than letting thought think you.

Sixteen
OUT OF THE BOX AND INTO THE FIELD

You must accept the truth from whatever source it comes.
— Moses Ben Maimon.

"Enlightenment" is simply a description of what happens when you see beyond your mind-made box and realize yourself as the field that contains all boxes. This field is the deeper truth that includes everything. This is the One.

It is easy to get comfortable within your own religion, tradition, method, or program. A spiritual seeker often derives his sense of self from his particular religion, tradition, method or program. He then lives, metaphorically speaking, within a box which conceals his awareness from seeing the deeper truth of life. If a particular religion, tradition, method, or program is being used to exclude, divide, cause conflict, or enhance a sense of self and separateness from other groups or people, then it is not truth. If it is not about truth, it is about you and your separation from those who do not confirm your mind-made sense of self.

The real truth cannot be grasped by the intellect. Be willing to open your mind widely so that you realize that you are not what you think or believe. You are much more than a tape recording of conditioning and memory, which must defend itself against other tape recordings. You are not a religion, tradition, method, or program. In those moments when you feel the urge to defend your religion, tradition, method, or program, you are only defending your own conditioning and memory—your own box, which is ego. Thinking completely within the box of your own religion, tradition, method, or program keeps you from realizing Oneness.

The deepest spiritual truth is much deeper and all-encompassing than any particular box. It does not need your defense. It does not come in a particular form or box. It includes all form as well as formlessness. Formlessness is the essence of who you are. It is consciousness itself. It is sometimes called "spirit." But these are all just words, presently arising thoughts that point beyond themselves to the truth of who you are. This truth cannot be named without smothering it. Once you grasp onto a thought or belief about the truth, you are ignorant of it. The fragment cannot see the whole.

You cannot touch spirit or hold it, but you know unmistakably that it is there. It is the very life that you are. So the truth, in order to be true, must include not just thought (form) but also essence (formlessness). Truth must ultimately see that no words, thoughts, beliefs, programs, religions, methods, or traditions could ever capture it. The truth is this essence within which these things arise and fall. It is the essence which is reading this book.

This essence within you can see your conditioning and memory operating. This is radical. This is what presence does, and what it is. It allows you to see how you are deriving a sense of self from what you think, and then separating yourself from others who do not confirm who you think you are. And when this realization happens, you realize there is no you, nor is there any religion, tradition, method, or program, except as a dream of thought, which is a dream of separation.

Thought may resist what is being said here. You may even find yourself getting angry when you read this book, especially if it is challenging some position you are holding. That is fine. But be very honest with yourself. Mature spirituality demands honesty above all else. Your anger is there for one reason only: to show you that you have been deriving a false sense of self from your religion, tradition, method, or program. The self is the energy that emphasizes a viewpoint, creating conflict in your life. It doesn't have to be a viewpoint associated with religion or spirituality. It could be a viewpoint about philosophy, politics, science or any other human endeavor or field. It could be simply a viewpoint about yourself or a friend or spouse.

An Illustration

Although words and concepts cannot grasp this ultimate truth, they can point to it. For example, look at the horizontal line below with the points A, B, and C on it.

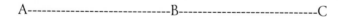

"A" represents the mind-identified state, where the mind is attached to thought, or identified with form. It relies almost exclusively on its belief systems for a sense of self, separating itself from others and other belief systems and opposite views. As nondual presence is realized, "A" moves all the way to "C" so to speak. This can happen gradually, or all it once. "C" represents that "place" of pure formlessness where concepts do not arise or are seen as false or illusory. But don't leave this in the notion of formlessness. Just remain open. Let this include form, which just means don't fall for the trap of creating a false division between formlessness and form. "B" represents a balance between form and formlessness. "B" is the living reality of Oneness beyond the experience of it. "B" is liberated from arguing about the One or God. Yet when arguing or disagreeing occurs, it is fully allowed. "B" is liberated from points of reference. It is free, even from wanting to be free, from caring whether others believe it is free, or believing that others need to be free. It is free from the notion that it is enlightened, or awakened, or any other point of reference. Yet it is free to use those words to point.

"B" is the opening in which experiences, states, feelings, words, points, thoughts, religions, beliefs and everything else happens or does not happen. Everything that happens within the open space is seen to be inseparable from the space itself. "B" is the liberation where one realizes that formlessness is her essence. Although she does not attach to form or thought, she also does not deny form or suppress thought. She also does not stay stuck in the identity of being pure formlessness. She is stuck in neither form nor formlessness. Any denial of the all-encompassing truth causes suffering in some way. Nothing is pushed away. Words are used freely, but without believing that the words are the truth. She is not looking for silence, presence, enlightenment, the awakened state, or God. She sees that those are only concepts pointing to the inexpressible truth all around and within her. There is no center. No point of reference. All seeking ends. There is only 'This' which includes it all. Everything is 'This.' In this liberation, there is either thought or no thought and no preference for either. "B" is in alignment with what is. Perfect acceptance of life in all it's appearances.

This is what the enlightened teachers have been pointing to for thousands of years. Buddha talked about the Middle Way, which is "B"—the living realization of this balance between form and formlessness. Zen masters speak of the harmonization between matter and spirit.

All of that is conceptual, however, and does not truly capture the truth to which it points. The "truth" is freedom itself, including freedom from any fixed point of view. The entire conceptualization above arises and falls within the essence to which it is pointing. The truth is accessible right now from where you stand. It is a pathless truth. It is now. It is what you are. You do not have to do anything, except notice what is already being done. What is already being done is that the mind is telling stories of separation. Notice all the thoughts that arise to tell you that there are divisions in life. See them for what they are: thoughts only. Let them pass without emphasizing them. That seeing is a present seeing. It is a timeless truth.

"B," in the Illustration above, is in no way a fixed point of reference. "B" is liberation. It is openness or love itself, which does not reject religions, traditions, methods, paths or programs. It sees it all as itself, so it includes every perspective, seeing no divisions ultimately.

Liberation sees that religions and traditions are never actually in conflict. There is only ever a dream of separation happening within the human mind. The eye of liberation sees that religions do not fight wars. Egos do. It is one-mind made self arguing with another mind-made self, which collectively amounts to one belief system fighting another. Liberation transcends but includes all religions and traditions, realizing itself as the one light of truth permeating all of them. At the same time, liberation sees that attachment to any one of them (as the sole truth) is merely delusion and a source of suffering, conflict, and division on earth.

Once this clarity arises, the whole notion of totally separate boxes out there in the world is seen as a mental illusion. Liberation no longer sees life through the distorted and self-centered prism of a box. It respects and nurtures any religion or tradition (box) that has the capacity to move an individual from the egoic view to the liberated view. But it is liberated from attachment to any box. Simply put, it sees that attachment is the dream self. Conflict between belief systems begins as attachment in the mind and is then projected outward as a dream. The holy war is within. In the realization that separation and conflict are products of the inward movement of mind, it is also realized that the healing of this dream of separation and conflict must also come from within. As the 13th Century Sufi poet Rumi said: "Out beyond ideas of wrongdoing and rightdoing there is a field. I'll meet you there. When the soul lies down in that grass, the world is too full to talk about." This field is already within you. It is love.

Love Is Truth

Love Does Not Want Anything in Return,
Only You Do.

— Scott Kiloby

Seventeen
TRUE LOVE DOES NOT RECOGNIZE ME AND YOU

Love is patient and kind; love does not envy or boast; it is not arrogant or rude. It does not insist on its own way; it is not irritable or resentful; it does not rejoice at wrongdoing but rejoices with the truth.

— *1 Corinthians 13*

Come out of the circle of time and into the circle of love.

— *Rumi*

In recognizing non-duality, the "me" vanishes. Poof. Gone. True love takes the place of the "me." This love was always here, but obscured by the movement of the dream self. In this recognition, the "me" is devoured by the full weight of this love, which is only concerned with what is true. To say that the "me" is devoured isn't accurate. The "me" was never really there. So it is seen for what it really is, an illusion.

This "true love" is not the sticky, attached, conditional, romantic love that the ego knows. The ego is the "me." This true love does not recognize "me" as real. The "me" could never have contained this completely open energy of true love. The "me" was too concerned with separation, self-protection, storytelling, self-centeredness, and resistance to what is. In the dream state, love would shine through in certain moments when the "me" faded away, but for the most part the "me" ruled the kingdom.

This true love is unconditionally open. It loves what is. It devours every illusion it meets, no matter what form the illusion takes. When this love finds the "me" irrelevant, it also sees through all by-products of the "me," including the need to separate, self-protect, resist, insist, be right, blame, debate, and hurt. It does not ignore these by-products, it simply knows that they emanate from a central illusion—"me." Love sees through the illusion. When it sees what appears as a "me" or "you" engaging in any of these activities, it knows that the doing comes from a misperception of separateness, a dream occurring in the mind.

Love loves itself everywhere it sees itself, and it sees itself everywhere, as itself. It loves and sees itself in the other person, the tree, the soda can, and the muddy pool of water after a rain. It knows that everything is One, and that this One is always here, already here, now, and nowhere else, at no other time. Love knows that any dividing of the One into parts is an attempt to understand the whole through its fragments. Hopeless. In that sense, this chapter is a hopeless—but loving— attempt to describe, through words, what is ultimately unknowable to the mind. The truth of which this speaks can only be known through the open energy of true love as it lives, and moves, moment to moment.

Although love sees every thought reflecting the dream of separation in space and time, it only recognizes and resonates with truth, which is that there is One Life, happening only now. In a way that this author cannot explain, love is truth. And love is appearing as everything.

Love does not recognize separateness in space. It does not split itself in two. It does not see the other as the "other." It only sees itself pretending to be an "other." So when you speak to this love from within the dream of separation, it does not recognize "you." It only recognizes love. It may find the dream of you to be funny, or somewhat sad or even tragic, but mostly it sees irrelevance—not because it does not care but rather because it cares very deeply. After all, it is love. What could care more deeply than love itself? It, however, cares only about what is true. And "you" are not seen as true as a separate person. The greatest love is to realize that suffering does not exist outside the dream of thought. Truth is, "you" were never there. You may not know this. Love knows. "You" and "me" are the last to know. An inexpressible truth is that the complete realization of human love can only be known in the absence of "you" and "me."

Love only exists now. Thus, it does not split itself in two temporally either. So love sees any attempt by the mind to reference a self in the past or future as an illusory movement away from what is true. Love does not resist or control. Thus, it does not seek to control or resist what is happening now. It knows that what is happening now is what is, which is the truth. This temporal dream manifests in various forms, such as: I was happier before; yesterday was worse than today; yesterday was better than today; that should not have happened; this should not be happening now; this should be happening now; I should be happy now; I should not be sad now; he should change; she shouldn't change; something should happen; something should not happen; tomorrow will be better; or tomorrow will be worse.

This is why suffering occurs. The dream (time, thought) gets mistaken for reality (now, love). Suffering is just part of the dream of "me." These movements of thought are illusory attempts to control and change what happened, what is now, and what should be. Love sees these movements as attempts by the mind to separate from and therefore to defy truth. An impossibility. And so it swallows these illusory movements, because they are not true. It does not ignore these forms or movements, it just recognizes them as false. The dream. They were always false. The only forms that believed they were true were the dreamy "me" and "you."

Love finds these stories about yesterday, tomorrow, and resistance to this moment to be irrelevant. Love, as truth, can only be fully revealed through total surrender to what is, in this moment.

When love totally devours the illusion of "me," the "me" is no longer acting. Love is. Unlike the "me," love does not seek result, reward, or gain. It sees those as evidence of the dream. The "me" attempts to usurp love for its own personal gain. The "me" wants some future return for its actions. The "me" expects love back. It does not know unconditional love. Love does not recognize the conditions that the "me" places on reality. Love wants nothing in return, only "you" and "me" do.

This awakened love does not discriminate. It does not prefer one form over the other. This is surely what Jesus meant when he said, "Love your enemy." He must have known that love has no enemies, only "you" do. So he is telling you that both "you" and your "enemies" are part of your dream and that loves sees through the dream. He is simply saying, be who you truly are. You are not a "me" or a "you." Those are masks. You are love. Jesus was trying to tell you that God is love and that you are not separate from love or from anything else.

Eighteen
LOVE IS ALREADY HERE

'This' is a wide open space, with enough room for an entire world, pulsating with a radical and unconditional love that will never be grasped by a mind locked in the search for something more.

— Jeff Foster

Take a moment to sit back and watch your mind. If you look deeply for one moment, you get a glimpse into the quiet mind. You open up the space of awareness within you, which is who you really are. This space contains a love that devours who you think you are. The quiet love of this space permeates your whole being. It permeates all of life. It is prior to any thought, including any thought about this quietness. It was here when you were born before the self-centered story began to obscure it. It is always here under the story.

If you are like most humans, you have been stuck in the noise of the story your whole life. This is why life is a struggle. The busy mind never quite touches reality. It merely interprets and thinks about it, usually for the benefit of a noisy, thought-based self that sees itself as the center. The quiet mind, however, is fully in touch with the reality underneath this noisy story. This quietness naturally includes the whole of life. The quiet mind, one could say, is love itself. It has no center.

One day I received an inspiring email from a friend which captured this spiritual truth better than I ever could.

The email contained actual answers by four- to eight-year-old children to the question, "What is love?" One particular seven-year-old boy named Bobby answered, "Love is what's in the room with you at Christmas if you stop opening presents and listen." Bobby is connected to the Divine. He isn't confused like so many adults.

When Bobby says love is "in the room" he is pointing to this quietness that is prior to thought. It is prior to the Christmas presents. It is prior to any form, whether it be a physical form, a thought form, a feeling, a reaction, a label, a name, or any other "thing." "In the room" means that this love is already here within us, as well as around us, and is not separate from us. When you tap fully into this quietness within, you see that there is no distinction between within and without. It is all One. And it includes all these forms. All sorts of forms come from this quietness: thoughts, feelings, relationships, cars, jobs, promotions, achievements, and Christmas presents—the list goes on. But when the mind becomes preoccupied with these forms, there is no recognition of love, which is formless. One could say, we push God out completely, in favor of our own self-centeredness.

When you watch your mind deeply, the incessant mental activity stops, even if only for a moment. You are mentally at rest. There is peace. Quietness. You have tapped into what Bobby has tapped into. That quietness is who you are. Rest there whenever you notice it. You are resting into your true nature. Watch thought as soon as it comes back in and that watching helps you to realize the quietness that is already here. Watching opens you up to the quietness—to the truth. Watch yourself as you become preoccupied with the Christmas presents, the car, the computer, and work. This means be aware of your preoccupation with thoughts about these things. Outside of thought, there is no such thing as ownership or possession of things. In becoming aware of that preoccupation, you are listening, as Bobby would say, to what is already here, prior to all of that.

You realize your true nature as love. You see that you do not need to seek, find, or go out and get love. You do not need to demand it from others or even expect it. You cannot get, seek, find, demand, or expect what you already are. Through this self-realization, everything you do is infused with love. You do not need to do anything except notice that this love is already here. Just realize you are it. You are this vast, quiet room called "love."

Nineteen
THE WAY, NOT YOUR WAY

Look at the trees: They let the birds perch and fly, with no intention to call them when they come and no longing for their return when they fly away. If peoples' hearts can be like the trees, they will not be off the Way.

— *Langya*

Langya was referencing the Tao Te Ching, translated as "The Book of the Way," written by Lao-tzu some 2,500 years ago. Tao means "The Way." Langya was speaking of the enlightened way of being, a way that is in alignment with reality or God. Jesus also spoke of this alignment in his own words in Matthew 6:

Therefore I tell you, do not worry about your life, what you will eat or drink; or about your body, what you will wear . . . Who of you by worrying can add a single hour to his life . . . See how the lilies of the field grow. They do not labor or spin.

What does it mean for your heart to be like the trees, and your mind to be like the lilies? For your heart to be like the trees, you must be detached. Detachment is sometimes misunderstood to mean apathy. Spiritual detachment is not the sense of not caring, or giving up. It is the exact opposite. You care deeply, but you care about all of life, not just the parts that suit you or benefit you in some way. You do not care because you think it is "the right thing to do" or because this book implies that you should care. You care in the way an arm cares about a leg when it is bleeding. The arm does not prefer the leg over the neck. It does not reach down to care for the leg because it will get something in return for its action. It does not ask the leg if it can help. It reaches down to the leg because the arm and the leg are One. They are not separate.

Spiritual detachment is the escape from your self-centered, sticky attachment to particular things and people that give you something in return or benefit you into a genuine love for what is.

In the egoic, self-centered dream in which most humans live, you believe that your love is derived from a particular form (i.e. an object or person). You love the beautiful snow-covered mountains, and the pretty woman in the grocery store, but you could care less for the trash in the garbage can, the ugly, old wallpaper in the bathroom, and the homeless guy who smells of liquor and cigarettes. Your heart becomes attached only to those things from which you believe you will benefit in some way or from which you will derive a greater sense of self. You mistakenly believe these things "give" you your love. How can something give you what you already are? Do you see that you are love? This love is beyond your story that life should benefit you or give you something.

In the egoic dream, the mind engages in a complicated categorization process, dividing up life into those things that give you pleasure and those that give you pain or do nothing for you. As the spiritual teacher Nisargadatta Maharaj put it: "The dream is not your problem. Your problem is that you like one part of your dream and not another. Love all or none of it, and stop complaining."

You love the sense of awe you experience when you look at that great big beautiful, snow-peaked mountain. But you are not particularly fond of the gravel alley behind your house.

You love the way a sense of recognition and delight bubbles into your whole being as the preacher or the spiritual teacher within your own religion uses words with which you can identify or speaks to beliefs you already hold. But you grimace and squirm a little inside when someone from another religion or method begins to speak about his, very different, belief system.

You love the pleasure your body feels as you indulge in warm, chocolate chip cookies, or drugs and alcohol, or whatever your vice may be. But you are irritated at the lady next to you in the park who insists on lighting a cigarette, or the child in the room who indulges in loud, abrasive screaming as she joyfully chases the other children around the room.

You love the feeling of being right when discussing politics with your friend. But you feel diminished, less than, and defensive when someone appears to show you that your position is wrong.

You love it when your partner lets you know that you are the sweetest, smartest guy she knows. But you feel at least a little bit of jealousy as she seems to warm up a little too much to the handsome guy in the room.

You love it when the day is warm and earth has blossomed into magnificent colors in the middle of May. But the dead, harsh cold of winter does not do much "for you." Quite frankly, you get irritated if you have to scrape the ice off of your car window.

Do you see the self-centered nature of the egoic dream? It wants what it wants, when it wants it, and how it wants it. And this is the cause of suffering. The ego is not concerned with reality. It is only concerned with keeping its self-centered dream alive. It is demanding, controlling, and interested mainly in its own pleasure. It likes to play God.

It seeks to recreate past pleasures, and avoid those things that appear to bring pain or bring nothing at all. It is always looking to gain. It mistakenly believes that the pain and pleasure, and the good and bad are somehow "out there" in things. It does not realize that the egoic mind is projecting the attributes of pain and pleasure, and good and bad onto these things. The mind is merely a projector. And the world is a reflection of the mind.

In the egoic state, when you look at something and label it as "bad," you do not see that it is only your label. You place it over the person or thing, usually because the labeling itself benefits you in some way. You are pointing into the dream that you create with thought, not seeing that it is your dream.

In this state, everything is about you—whether you like or dislike something, whether something does or does not suit you, whether you agree or disagree with the other, whether something is or is not beautiful to you. The labeling of good and bad keeps the self in place. There is nothing wrong with having likes and dislikes. But when the labeling is identified with completely such that you derive your sense of self from it, suffering and separation arise. Billions of people are walking the earth concerned mainly for themselves, wondering why the earth is being destroyed, and why there is so much war, conflict, drug use, poverty, and so forth. Until the mind sees that it is projecting these things into the world, and that the problem is not "out there," no true transformation can happen.

Realize deeply that the entire interplay between the law of opposites (good vs. bad, having vs. not having, you vs. me, us vs. them, pain vs. pleasure) arises within the space of who you are. You are not any one of the forms which happen to be arising in this space.

True Gratitude and Love Are Beyond the Dream of Self

To be a lover of what is, is to have a heart like the trees—a heart for which no words could ever completely capture its love, but that loves to express itself anyway. This heart loves the coming and the going of everything equally. This love is realized only in that field beyond the ideas of "good" vs. "bad" and "right" vs. "wrong" to which the egoic mind clings. This field includes it all.

In this field, you love it when the bird comes, and you love it when it flies away. You have no preference. You are simply grateful to be here watching whatever it does. Not grateful in the sense that you can tell all your friends how grateful you are. Not grateful in the sense that you try to convince yourself that you are grateful by thinking about birds. No, this grateful is simply grateful for what is. In fact, it is not that you, as a separate person, are grateful. Gratitude simply is, when the self-centered you is not seeking something from the situation. So when the bird is not around, gratitude is grateful for that. It does not try to recreate a past experience of gratitude. It does not long for the bird. It simply loves what is—whatever is.

You cannot obtain love from an object or person. You are love. So although it appears that you are interacting with something separate from yourself, and in which you believe you will find or experience love, what is really happening is that love is interacting with itself. No subject. No object. Just love. So to say that one aspect of this One Life is better or more favorable than another is simply your dream.

To love "what is" means to love it when your dog jumps up on your lap, but also when she jumps down, more interested in the bone on the floor than your attention. It means that it does not matter whether you bought this book or not. This love knows that the truth is not in these words. The truth is life itself.

To love "what is" means to love the brilliant, inviting smells of a Thanksgiving dinner as it sits on the table waiting to be eaten, and also the stack of dirty dishes piled up by the sink after dinner.

This love loves when you are about to go see a movie you have been wanting to see for months, but also loving it when it is over.

This love loves it when the doctor gives you a clean bill of health, but also when she says you must stay in bed for weeks to recover from the flu.

This love loves it when your spouse listens to every word of a story you are telling about work, but also when she turns away, apparently bored of the details.

This love loves life and death. It does not make a problem out of either. This is not a callous disregard for life. This is a celebration of it. It the realization that we are much, much more than individual bodies and stories.

The ego knows nothing of the true Way, which is to live and die as the trees and lilies do. They live and die without problem and without effort. They neither labor, worry, nor spin. The ego is shoulder-deep in laboring, worrying, and spinning.

If you are not living in alignment with the Way, you may mistakenly believe that, if you do not resist what is happening, life will fall apart. You may believe that you must think about things, to decide what is good and what is bad and take action according to your thought—not realizing that this merely strengthens the illusion of separation. This is the ultimate self-centeredness, to believe that the very existence of good somehow depends upon your thought. Do you see that you are the arm? Do you see that the idea that the arm must think about whether to help the suffering leg is self-centered madness?

Love is the natural state. It simply is. It simply does what it does, regardless of our attempts to control it, understand it, think about it, expect it, or take credit for it.

The Way, mentioned by Langya, and by so many other spiritual teachers, is a way of being in this moment, in a state of complete non-resistance. Whatever action needs to be taken, it is not taken from the egoic, self-centered dream. It is taken from this Way, which is in alignment with reality. It is taken on behalf of the whole, not the self.

To find this Way, do nothing. Just notice that it is already here. Allow curiosity to be open to what is appearing in front of you, no matter what it is. Do not try to convince yourself that it is "good" or "bad." No, look at it. See the essence of it. Allow your awareness to see it for what it is. Then watch any judgments that rise up within you, either through thought or emotion, to resist what is, or to tell stories about it. Face whatever arises directly.

Be as an empty vessel, so that God may work through you. As Meister Eckhart expressed: "To be full of things is to be empty of God. To be empty of things is to be full of God." Do not get caught up in your concepts of God or your concepts of any other thing in life. Use your conceptual mind at work, to fix your car, learn a new skill, or put your child's toy together, and then come back to this moment, which is the only place where life is. Life in this moment is naturally free, clear, peaceful, intelligent, compassionate and loving.

The Way is love. But it is not the sticky, attached self-centered love to which the ego is accustomed. This is a love for the whole, for what is. It is a love for life. You are that life. In this moment, through complete presence, you simply allow life to work through you. You are no longer at odds with life. You are like the lilies in the field, like the trees mentioned by Langya. You neither labor nor toil nor worry. You neither demand nor resist nor know. All that is left is this Way, this pure loving space, unencumbered by the pettiness of you and all your self-centered efforts. This is what is meant by the phrase, "Thy will be done."

Twenty
THE SPACE OF LOVE

When you receive whoever comes into the space of Now as a noble guest, when you allow each person to be as they are, they begin to change.

— *Eckhart Tolle*

Notice what happens within your body and mind when a loved one says something hurtful or something you strongly disagree with, or does something that irritates you. There is sometimes a contraction, a coiling up, as if you are a snake about to attack.

Are you expecting this book to give you a prescription which you can use to avoid feeling that contraction? No, the message of this entire book could be summed up in one word: "Notice." Noticing means feeling and seeing directly the contraction in the moment it arises. Acceptance happens naturally in that noticing. Love heals from within. If that is a prescription, so be it. But there is nothing this book can give you that you do not already have. You are the awareness to which the book points.

Acceptance does not mean agreeing mentally with something someone says or does. Agreement and disagreement is so often stuck in the egoic realm. True acceptance means being the space for someone. Only presence accepts. Presence is the space of love.

When I say "the space of love" I am speaking of going inward. Here is an illustration: imagine yourself sitting on the hood of a car on a starry night. You are waiting to see a falling star. You know that if you turn your attention away from the sky at any moment, you might miss the falling star. This is very alert attention. Watch your mind and your inner body when you are relating to others. By going inward, you recognize that your essence and your loved one's essence are the same energy, the same space. When your attention is on this inward space, love is realizing itself.

Breathe in and feel this loving invitation from Eckhart Tolle:

> Can you feel the subtle energy field that pervades the entire body and gives vibrant life to every organ and every cell? Can you feel it simultaneously in all parts of the body as a single field of energy? . . . . The more attention you give it, the clearer and stronger this feeling will become. . . . Feel the inner body even when engaged in everyday activities. Feel the stillness deep inside it. Keep the portal open.

Eckhart is pointing to the space of love that is already within you. Here is an exercise to help you realize this inward space. Place one hand on your chest and another on your stomach. Close your eyes and take your hands off. How would you find your inner chest and stomach without using your hands or eyes? Let your inner awareness find that space. This space is who you are. The space is finding itself.

By going inward, you realize that your outward interpretation of the world is merely a projection of your own mind. It is your dream. Your mind is simply projecting a dream that people and situations ought to be different than the way they are. When you believe that your loved one should be different than the way she is, you are not relating to your loved one at all. You are relating to an ideal or image in your head. You are having a relationship with your own thoughts. Reaching into your own dream to try to fix or argue with your loved one is like trying to fix or argue with pixels on a movie screen projected from your own mind. It is not true that your loved one should be the way you want her to be. She should be exactly the way she is because that is who she is in this moment. The space of love realizes itself in that seeing.

By realizing yourself as this inner space, you see clearly that thoughts about yourself and about others arise within this space. This space is here, always, as who you are. It was here when you were two years old, and it will be here on your deathbed. Thoughts and emotions come and go within the space. Do not hold on to any of them. Watch them arise and fall in this space. This space does not come and go. It is changeless and timeless.

Notice the thoughts and emotions arising when you want to attack your loved one or defend yourself, then notice the second layer of thought and emotional resistance that tells you that you should not be thinking or feeling whatever you are thinking and feeling in this moment. This second layer of judgment is the ego coming in through the back door, so to speak. This is the spiritual search. It wants to convince you that something should be happening other than what is happening. That is insane. You are not the first layer of thoughts and emotions, the conditioning that wants to attack or defend. You are also not the second layer of judgment coming through to judge and rationalize that first layer. You are the space in which all of this is happening. Notice what is watching this whole interplay. It is something very subtle. There is a silent watcher deep within. That is who you are and that is who your loved one is.

Can you be the space in which your loved one is talking, in which the words are arising and falling? It is funny to even say, "Can you be the space," because you already are the space. The question is, "Do you realize this?" Do you see and feel this with your whole being? Notice what happens within you when you want to attack your loved one or defend yourself in response to something he or she says. Can you be the space in which even your own reaction arises and falls?

Notice any thoughts or emotions of resentment in your body. Do not try to rationalize them or bring about their end. Become fully aware of them. Resentment has nothing to do with the person you resent. It is the dream self keeping self-centeredness in place. You are simply telling yourself a story that life should be the way you want it to be. Can you sense the space in which these thoughts and emotions of resentment arise? You are that space, not the energy of resentment within it.

Many times when we are reacting, it is as if awareness is asleep within the mind and body. But awareness is never asleep. It has simply become entangled in the thoughts and emotions arising within it. This leads to the mistaken belief that you are separate from the rest of life. Enlightenment or presence just means allowing the light of awareness to be aware of itself, so that all reactions are seen in the moment they arise. This light sees the falseness of outward pointing into the dream. Judgments strengthen the dream of separation. Do not suppress judgments, just see them.

Notice the inward. The inward is your inner body and mind that is the space in which everything happens. Watch any disagreement which arises within your own mind. Allow yourself to be the space within which even agreement and disagreement arise and fall.

If you need to assert yourself to your loved one, explain how his or her behavior is hurting you or otherwise respond, your response is coming from this space of love. This is surrendered action. It only happens in your absence. So do not try to manufacture this space. Love cannot be manufactured. There is nothing you can do to bring it about because love already is the natural state, underneath all your efforts. Actions from this space carry a completely different energy than the "attack and defend" energy of ego. If your spouse continues to attack you, simply say "thank you." "Thank you for telling me who you are and what is important to you." Then feel the hurt within you, if there is any. That hurt is waking you up from the dream of separateness.

It takes only one person to welcome presence into a relationship for that relationship to be transformed. When one dream self dissolves, there is nothing for the other dream self to attack or defend itself against. The space of love that is left upon this dissolution is who you and your loved one truly are beyond your mental stories of each other. These stories are the cause of conflict. There is a tendency here to say that this space is the deeper love that connects you as One. But, more pointedly, in this space beyond the stories, it is realized that there never was a disconnection. There was only a dream. When you realize yourself as this space, and you are looking into the eyes of your loved one, you realize that you are looking at yourself. The One is realizing itself.

Liberation from the Dream of Separation

*Love is picnicking with a peanut butter and jelly
sandwich under the shade of an oak tree while
everyone else is searching for——or claiming to have
found——God or Enlightenment.*

– Scott Kiloby

Twenty-one
THIS SEAMLESS ONE

God said to Moses, "I AM THAT I AM"

— *Exodus 3:14*

There is no becoming. ALL IS.

— *Wei Wu Wei*

The eye through which I see God is the same eye through which God sees me: my eye and God's eye are one eye, one seeing, one knowing, one love.

— *Meister Eckhart*

There is only One. There is not ever in any sense many, or even two.

— *David Carse*

There are no separate things. There is only this seamless One. 'This.' God. This Oneness is sometimes called "non-duality" meaning "not two." There is no one here to think of anything which happens or does not happen within this One as a separate thing or event, until thought reaches up to try to be somebody. Once thought reaches up to be a "me" in relation to the rest of life, illusion arises. Thought reaches out of nothingness to grab onto some fragment within this One, to make the fragment separate from and more important than the whole. The mind divides this One into millions of other fragments. The dream self names and labels these fragments to know who it is in relation to everything else.

This self continues in its illusion only as long as it attaches to one problem after another, one concept after another, one thought after another, one self-deluded belief after another. This attachment creates a conceptual cloud that obscures reality. The self misses the utter beauty and simplicity of the whole.

When awareness becomes fully aware of itself and of this movement by thought to make a separate self, the mind-made story of a person dies. The thought-made entity is seen for what it is—nobody. There is nobody here. In that realization, the whole universe comes alive.

The words "the universe comes alive" arise within the dream. The universe has always been alive. To be more accurate, awareness—once the cloud of delusion has been lifted—sees the aliveness of the universe. It sees itself as that universe. Awareness sees through its fixation on thought, on self. But to even pretend as if the words "It sees itself as the universe" is the truth deadens the seamless vastness of 'This' and turns it into a concept. Although concepts are inseparable from this seamless One, it is so easy to get lost in the fragmented conceptual cloud, and miss the One–the actual. The actual is where this utter mystery is. It is where the truth is. The actual is realized only now.

Books and teachings point you to the truth, using concepts. The actual truth must be seen and realized. It is beyond the concepts that are pointing to it. I was recently in a group Satsang setting. Everyone was sitting around the room reading a teacher's written words. There was no teacher in the room. Noses were buried in books, coming up for air only to reference something they had read, and to talk about "what that meant." "What was the teacher saying?" "What did he mean there?"

Noses buried in books.

Minds buried in words and teachings.

Buried in the conceptual, in the fragments.

Missing the actual. 'This.'

I wanted to say to everyone, "Stop. Look around. Don't you see? 'This' is it! 'This' is what you are looking for. You can't leave it. You are it. If you bury your head too much in that teaching, you miss it completely." I didn't say anything though. It was realized that there are no others to awaken. It feels funny to have even written this book—to have realized that there is no self to awaken, only to write a book that appears to teach the illusory others about waking up.

If there is anything to teach, it is not to become dependent on the dream teaching or the dream teacher. Use them as tools. Let them free awareness from its attachment to the dream, letting it expand to see everything within and without as one seamless whole. Then let awareness burn the tools themselves up. The truth burns up everything that is false.

Noticing the Seamlessness

When you are done reading here, sit back in your chair—or walk around. It does not matter. Notice the vast space in every direction, embracing you intimately. Notice the space around your fingers, around your body, and around every object you see. Everything is showing you the seamlessness between objects and space. This is the One. You are it. In a way that the intellect will never grasp, the space and the objects are not separate.

Notice that this vast space is also within you. You are that space. There is no beginning and no ending of "you." The space is one seamless space within and without. So where is this separate you? If you allow the question to open awareness up more, untangling it from thought's need to answer, the question dissolves into the space from which it arose. From where did the question arise? Where did it go? It arose from the space and dissolved back into it. But to even place words upon that leads the mind to think it "gets it." There is nothing to get and no one here to get it. The notion that "thought arises from space and dissolves back into it" is just another thought that "arises from space and dissolves back into it." This is why one thought leads to another, one fragment to another. This is why thought will not see 'This.' 'This' is seen only in the absence of the thought-based self that is trying to see it.

When thought arises, notice that you cannot see the beginning of it. There is a seamlessness between thought and the space from which it appears to arise. Thought smoothly bleeds out of awareness and back into awareness. Or, an oscillation happens between thought and awareness. This seamlessness is showing you that it is all One.

But is it even true that "thought arises from space and dissolves back into it"?

What is thought and what is space? These are human concepts. They are the past, coming up to meet this moment. The mind sees an apparent distinction between form and formlessness, a distinction that should be respected. After all, the words, "all form is formlessness," don't seem to ring true as you are getting run over by a semi-truck. But the truck arose from formlessness, too, and will dissolve back into it, whatever "it" is.

This body/mind that you call "me" will go back to where it came from upon physical death. But because the body/mind is not separate from that which it came from, it does not truly go anywhere. Why are you afraid of death? Death is just the end of the story. But the story is not real anyway. Where are you going to go? Your personal story dies, but who you really are cannot be killed. You are life. You are 'This.' The whole seamless process of conception, birth, growth, death, and decomposition is showing you the seamlessness.

Every form arises and dissolves back into that which it came. There is one seamless movement from nothing— to the appearance of something (thought, truck, you)— to nothing. But even to say "nothing" or "something" leads the mind to believe that it knows something about which it is speaking. To even say that form arises from formlessness is misleading. Form and formlessness are dancing as one seamless interplay. No beginning and no end. No separation. Form is formlessness. Formlessness is form. Only thought makes a distinction.

There is only nothingness appearing as everything. There is a dream of separation. Yet there is also only One Life. Each of these expressions is pointing to the same truth. This truth is radically inexpressible yet words keep arising within it. The mind cannot grasp 'This.' It tries, but all it ever comes up with are fragments—the endless categorizing and describing of parts. So the only real fragmentation, the only real separation is in thought, in the conceptual. No such fragmentation or separation exists in the actual.

So, where are you going to go today? Are you going to go to the supermarket or maybe the park? No matter where you go, you are still in the One. You are it. You cannot leave yourself. And so you are alone in it—as it. You are energy, and you are seeing yourself everywhere, in a magnificent and ordinary array of forms. No matter how much thought would like to believe that this place is a supermarket or a park, those are only thoughts—little stories of what is. This "separate you" is an illusion, too. These stories will never see the whole.

You cannot seek the One because you are it. This realization is not something you can make happen. All movements to bring it about will only obscure the realization. One glance at it, just for a moment, is enough to show you the whole truth of it. Instead of searching for it, which is absurd because you are it, simply be with what is arising now. The searching arises from the thoughts, "I do not have it," or "I do not see it." The spiritual search could be described as wanting to see something other than what you already see.

Here is a little story of my two dogs that illustrates the insanity of searching for what is already and always here, now. One day, I had just a handful of ground hamburger left in my plate after lunch. I decided to feed it to my two dogs. I placed it in Josie's bowl, when she was not watching. I then went into the next room to place the rest of it in Mai-Ling's bowl. Josie came running towards Mai-Ling's bowl, searching for the ground beef she had been smelling for the last twenty minutes. The two growled at each other. Josie did not realize that there was beef in her bowl. I had to drag her back to her bowl to show it to her. Once she realized it was there, she was satisfied. That is what the spiritual seeker does. He searches for the truth in every place but his own bowl—in drugs, jobs, relationships, sex, food, books, teachers, religions, methods, and practices. He looks in every place it would not be. Once he directs his attention inward and to this moment, there it is. He sees that it was always here. The search simply obscured it. Noticing what is in this moment has a totally different energy than the energy of the time-based search.

Notice how you are deceiving yourself about the truth. You are looking for it in thought rather than in reality. Do you see the bookshelf across the room? No, you don't. That is not a bookshelf. You are interacting only with your own thought "bookshelf." That thought is what makes you feel separate from this "other" thing called a bookshelf. Look more closely—without mental commentary, without the thought "bookshelf" or "books." If that or any other thought arises, just watch it and then let it die on its own. It will. Like all forms, it is temporary and does not even exist as anything separate from anything else, including from wherever it came.

If you look, without thought, there is no you. There is only looking. Even that is a story, a commentary.

But this looking allows you to see the seamlessness of 'This.' No ending and no beginning. No person, and no bookshelf. Just a brilliantly simple mystery, far beyond anything the mind can understand. Take that looking everywhere. Notice your hand as it reaches for a glass with tea or coffee in it. Notice that the mind just made this stuff up—the notion that there is a hand, reaching, to something called a glass, to drink, something called tea or coffee. It's a wonderful story, but is it true?

There is one seamless movement involved in drinking that tea, and no one there drinking it. But to even say that is a story. No matter what we say about 'This,' our words are only telling a story about it. Our noses are buried in the conceptual. As a writer, I have the paradoxical task of using concepts to point you away from the conceptual and into the actual (which paradoxically includes the conceptual). Mind boggling, isn't it? Exactly. It is so mind boggling that the sooner you allow your mind to stop trying to "get it," the sooner it will be realized. 'This' loves to express itself, but it is only ever saying, "Jump off the expression into the realization to which it points."

'This' Is One Inseparable Love

'This' is the flower in the park, the blowing wind, the smell of barbecue pork chops in a grill, the dog poop near the bench, and the space around these "things" that seamlessly embraces them. These things are not at all separate from each other.

When there is a noticing that this self is not really here, as something separate from these things and from the rest of life, love becomes fully realized. But "you" don't realize it. You do not gain anything from it. This love swallows the separate you. It is that big. Just as with all aspects of this seamless One, there is no beginning and no ending to this love. It does not start here and end there. It is not only in this thing or that thing. It is not yours, and yet without you it could not be realized. You are that important, but not as a separate entity. No, you are the opening that allows this love to see itself everywhere, the opening in which the concept of "person" arises. This love is this space, this awareness, but it is also this body, these thoughts, that bookshelf.

In awakening into what is, even the words "love" and "One" lose their importance. There is only 'This.' 'This' is too full to talk about. But we will talk about it anyway because, in some strange and mysterious way, even words and concepts (when there is no longer a belief that they are pointing to separate things) are equally 'This,' as beautiful and important as anything else. Every thought, word and image arises inseparably within the awareness that sees it. See this for yourself. It may appear, at first, that thought arises within what you are, as if thought is something separate from what you are, awareness. But look again. Look for the line dividing awareness from thoughts that arise in awareness. There is no line. If you find a line, it just means you have found another thought, another mental image.

See that everything, every thought, emotion, state, sensation, and experience, appears and disappears *inseparably* within the awareness that sees it. Seamlessness is everywhere. Inseparability is the nature of life. To even say that we are space or pure awareness only, somehow divorced from concepts, is to fragment 'This.'

'This' sees the seamlessness between form and formlessness and recognizes how futile it is to even try to describe 'This.' You are 'This.' To ever say that one fragment of the seamless One is more important than the other is the dream. Yet spiritual teachings will make the concepts "love," "One," and 'This' more important until it is realized that they are not. Those words are merely arising in 'This."

Or we could just go enjoy the barbecue or sit on the bench next to the dog poop. That would be 'This,' too.

Twenty-two
THE INWARD DEPTH

The most sublime truth of all has never been stated or written or sung. Not because it is far away and can't be reached, but because it is so intimately close, closer than anything that can be spoken.

— Gangaji

If a spiritual teaching works to speed up your mind, engage it intellectually, bring about the energy of agreement or disagreement, or send you searching into future for yourself, then either the teaching is not emanating from the spirit or your mind is stuck in the conceptual dream.

Words can carry such meaning to the mind. It may seem as if, when you are reading them, they are the truth. But the words, no matter how beautiful, whether they are from Gangaji or anyone else, are only pointing to the truth. Nobody owns this truth. It does not belong to spiritual teachers or those who seem to be able to express it more clearly than others. You are the truth. This is the truth that is "so intimately close, closer than anything than can be spoken."

So if this book spins your mind into agree/disagree mode, stop reading. A true spiritual teaching points you to this deeper, simpler truth of who you are. Not the time-based story in your head. That is thought. Although thought arises within who you are, you are not thought. It is more accurate to say that thought and you are not separate. But, because most humans are attached to what they think, and this causes the illusion of separation, this book speaks mainly to freeing consciousness from its attachment to thought.

Let the words of this and every spiritual book take you to a deeper place within you. When the words "One," "God," or 'This' are used here, I am pointing not only to the unending universe or space in every direction outside your body, but also to the deep space within you. There is a universe within you which is directly accessible through inner body awareness. The mind-made story of you will never see this.

Feel your inner body, and how it is inextricably connected to what is perceived as outward—"outside" of your body. You are alive and whole as One life, both within and without. This One life includes this inner peace, the deep well of love within you. Once you realize this depth inwardly, you see that there is no separation between what I am calling "inward" and "outward."

An Exercise in Depth

Try this exercise: on a piece of paper write the word "dog" and right next to that, draw a picture of a dog. Now, ask yourself, which of these is actually the dog?

Neither one, right? One is a word pointing to something and another is a drawing depicting something. Neither is actually this thing we call a dog. Now, go find your dog "Sally" and sit quietly with her. Now you have found a dog, right? No. You are merely interacting with your own thought. Somewhere along the way in life, you were told or you learned that this "thing" is a dog. So you began to associate the formulation of the following letters—D O G—with this utterly mysterious life sitting before you. But it could just have easily been called a "wallup." Then, you would be completely convinced while sitting with Sally that you know what a wallup is and that it is right there in front of you. Yet, in reality, you would still only be interacting with your own thought of "wallup." This is memory. Conditioning. Thought. Nothing else. Thought cannot show you the depth of anything. It stops you at the surface. It cannot show you the mystery. It cannot show you life, because it is in the business of denying life. It merely places a superficial label on something.

Now, keep sitting next to Sally and look deeply with your whole being at what you have been calling a dog. Put your hands on the dog. Feel her breathing. Feel your own breathing. Sally is not in control of her breathing. You are not in control of your breathing. Nor are you or Sally in control of your pumping hearts. Also, a large majority of your thoughts about Sally (e.g. her breed, where you bought her) is completely involuntary and a result of past conditioning. Feel the essence of life within Sally. Feel that same essence within yourself. This is the inward depth.

What is doing all this? What is pumping hearts, breathing, thinking, looking, living? It isn't you. Life is living itself through you, and through Sally, so to speak. But to even say that is to pretend as if the conceptual mind can grasp this. It cannot. Life is happening at a depth which is beyond thought.

There is a sort of unconscious arrogance in believing that thought, which is outward interpretation, can explain this inward depth of life. For example, you believe you know who your spouse is. You do not realize you are constantly engaging with your own story of your spouse, based in past conditioning, which is not who he or she is. You believe you know what everything is merely because you have placed thought upon it.

As you are sitting with Sally, your spouse, or anyone, watch any story that arises in your mind in some futile attempt to understand this mystery. These stories are blocking you from seeing and feeling the inward depth. These stories are relatively true on the level of mind. But if you only consult this superficial processor called thought in order to sense and understand life, the realization of the absolute, deeper truth of life will elude you. The absolute truth is unfathomable, and also absolutely accessible as the very life that you are in this moment. It is that which sees these stories.

'This' Cannot Be Threatened

The true nature of 'This' is much more mysterious, deep, loving, and beautiful than anything you think about it. Life is sacred. But "sacred" is just another thought. It is a great pointer and sounds very spiritual. But ultimately, that story too must die in order for you to see what is truly here, now—to see the true depth of who you are and the sacredness of 'This.' There is nothing wrong with the word "sacred." Use it. It is a beautiful word. But it is pointing to something infinitely more beautiful.

The stories that obscure the depth of life die naturally when you notice them. This was expressed eloquently in the book, *A Course In Miracles*:

Nothing real can be threatened.
Nothing unreal exists.
Therein lies the peace of God.

Once you grok the inward depth, you see that you are not separate from that which you call "Sally" and your spouse. To grok means to feel or know something with your whole being, to drink it into the depth of your heart. This knowing is beyond the level of conceptual understanding. It is much more intimate. It is so deep that it changes the way you view everything. When you look at either Sally or your spouse with this inward depth, you are looking at yourself, at life, beyond the stories and thoughts that describe it. Life is aware of itself. You are the vehicle in which that is happening. This is the inward depth of Oneness. When you realize it, it is unmistakable. It is the realization that there is a universe within you, and that same universe is within everything you see.

Someday your body, your spouse's body, and your dog's body will no longer be here. They are forms, which arise and fall within 'This.' But this depth, this animating principle of life, does not die. You cannot kill life. In seeing beyond the story of self, spouse, and Sally, there is a realization of a sacred depth which cannot be threatened in any way. You must die to the mental self in order to realize this and live fully. Seeing the depth of life frees you from your fear of death. When the fear of dying leaves, the fear of living leaves with it. The ego dies, but not because you desire its death. Only an ego would want to get rid of itself. It dies because it was always a dream. What is left is what is real. In this realization lies the peace of God.

Twenty-three
YOU – THE UNNAMABLE OPENING

A person is not a thing or a process but an opening through which the absolute manifests.

— Martin Heidegger

Now, allow Heidegger's statement to be forgotten. Forget it completely. Do not think about it. Do not try to remember it and share it with others. Do not contemplate it. It is gone. You read it and now you are reading this. Or, remember it, think about it, contemplate it, and share with others. This opening is that within which things either happen or do not happen. Do not make a problem out of the happening or not happening. Don't fixate on any aspect of reality. Just notice. The opening does the rest.

Heidegger's statement is not the opening. It is merely a pointer. It points you to the truth of who you are, an unnamable opening through which the entire universe is intelligently aware of itself. Yes, I just named it by saying it is an "unnamable opening." That is the paradoxical trap of the truth. Whenever we speak or think about this opening, concepts are necessary, yet no concept captures it. Concepts arise and fall within it. In fact, it is not even an "IT." It is not a thing. It is that which is prior to or beyond all things, and at the same time includes all things. Language makes the opening appear to be an object, because language contains the subject/object dichotomy. But things, nouns, verbs, subjects, and objects arise and fall within the opening. As David Carse says, "The truth exists, but cannot be expressed." Lao-tzu expressed this truth as, "The Tao that can be spoken is not the eternal Tao."

Confused yet? Perfect! Notice that within which confusion arises. That is the opening.

As far as pointers go, Heidegger's is about as good as it gets. It is very sharp. It is like a sign along the road that tells you as precisely as possible where this opening is. But the funny thing about pointers is that the truth is much closer than the pointer. It is so close that it is often missed. People spend lifetimes searching for the truth, struggling with notions of finding it or not finding it, losing it or not losing it. This struggle occurs because of a failure to realize that searching, finding, and losing are occurring within a dream of thought.

The truth cannot be lost or found. You are it.

When I say truth, I mean the opening to which Heidegger is pointing. When I say opening, I mean this immovable, deeply silent you which is realized when attachment to thought dissolves. It has been called the Source, the One, the Understanding, God, and the True Self. It will be described differently based on the particular conditioning describing it. But this "you" is certainly not the ego. The ego arises and dissolves within this opening. The opening is not any of these words. These words merely point to it.

Do you see the paradoxical trap yet? Using words to point to this opening can be tricky unless you realize with your whole being that words are like matter floating in space. You are like the opening within which the matter and the space present themselves. But the opening is not a thing. It is openness itself. And the minute you attempt to seek the truth by focusing solely on one bit of matter (e.g., a word or concept) or just the space, you divide your experience in two. A fragment of the truth cannot see the whole truth.

Traps

One trap is believing that you need to have a big spiritual experience in order to be free. When the word "awakening" is used in this book, it is not referring to an event in time. It is a present seeing. Some have a big awakening event and some don't. If you go looking for an experience in the future, you are solidifying ego. You are solidifying the story of time. Similarly, when the word "Oneness" is used in this book, it is not referring to the experience of Oneness or the moment of enlightenment where everything, including the dream of a separate self, falls away and you see yourself as the wall, the kitchen sink, and the cat. That is a 'road to Damascus' type experience. Don't fall for the trap of believing you need some future event to happen. Although this author had such an experience, I've talked to many who did not have a big experience. It simply isn't necessary.

Those who have a big experience call it "big" simply because, in the moment before the experience, separation seemed really true and real. The experience washed the sense of separation away in one swoop. It feels like a light switch suddenly turning on. The contrast between the dark and light is remarkable. Therefore, the experience itself is given more weight than it should have. Others experience more of a gradual falling away of the sense of separation. In their case, it is more like a dimmer switch slowly turning on. The result is the same: freedom from separation. And the "entry" point is always the present moment.

Another trap can arise if you do have a big experience. If the experience is overwhelming, you may fall into the trap of believing that *you* have attained a higher state of consciousness. But experiences, states, and everything else arise and fall within this opening. The Oneness experience is simply revealing that you, as a separate self, are an illusion which arises and falls within this opening called "One." The word "One" is therefore pointing to the opening. This opening is an absence of the self that would claim some egoic story about being enlightened or attaining something called "Oneness." It isn't an attainment at all. It's a loss. And in that loss there is perfect contentment, peace, and freedom with no need to try and own it on a personal level.

The opening is much closer and simpler than any experience or state that arises in it. The opening is sometimes called beingness. The word "One" simplifies the understanding and accounts for the fact that this opening includes it all. It includes the fact that the experience of Oneness happens within the opening. It also accounts for the experience of cleaning your toilet, which is just as true as any other experience. All experiences happen within this opening. The "opening" is not a thing the mind can wrap itself around. It is openness itself.

After an initial experience or insight into Oneness, thought may return to attempt to reconstitute a self. It may try to explain the awakening away as being less than a full awakening or not as thorough as the awakening of Buddha or Krishnamurti or some other teacher. That is fine. All doubt and explanations arise within this. But the explanation is the ego's attempt to return to the business of the dream self as if the truth had not been realized. It is running scared again. It may attempt to continue identifying with whatever job title or other roles or identities were in place prior to the awakening.

Rather than running away from the awakening, the ego may attempt to make a self out of the insights experienced in it. It may create a new belief system or believe that it is a spiritual teacher or a person who is awakened. Again, fear is fueling these thought movements. By seeking a false sense of mental certainty or believing thoughts that it is spiritually above others, thought is trying to protect itself from the pure love, vulnerability, innocence, and intimacy that are revealed in the awakening. These fear-based thoughts are illusions created by an ego which is running from the ultimate reality which devours it. Titles, roles, identities, fears, doubts, and explanations arise and fall within the opening.

There are other potential enlightenment pitfalls. For example, it is easy to get lost in the notion of formlessness, even to the point of vilifying form (e.g., words and concepts). One could even say, figuratively speaking, the ego becomes identified with the sense of being "formlessness." Ironically, the ego then creates duality within the world of non-duality. This is common in enlightenment or non-duality circles and website discussion groups. These egoic identities are the ones correcting everyone's language, badgering others to use non-dual words such as "pure awareness" or even "Oneness." They become fixated on the way something is expressed, on the particular words used, apparently believing that the truth can be expressed. David Carse discussed this pitfall in his book, *Perfect Brilliant Stillness*:

> One person says, "I'm glad you came." And the other answers, "Who? Who is glad?" And I think, the Advaita thought police never sleep. An old Ch'an master would give you a whap upside the head with his stick. What are you saying, 'Who is Glad?' She is glad, you dope, and she's being honest enough to tell you so.

The Advaita thought police, as he calls them, do not see that the whole notion of correcting, debating and challenging others on the level of language and thought is, by its very nature, identification with form. They miss the delightful inner contradiction between the realization that they are formlessness and this divisive identification with form. Whenever there is attachment to concepts, even concepts about Oneness, the separate self is operating.

Do you see the contradiction? Perfect. Do not seek clarity. Notice that within which the contradiction arises. That is the opening. If you are interested in the truth, here is a delicious opportunity: go find other statements in this book that apparently contradict what is being said here or go find other teachers, authors, religions, traditions, or belief systems that contradict this book.

Then recognize yourself as the opening within which all these contradictions arise. Teachers, students, seekers, teachings, traditions, religions, beliefs, contradictions, hairballs, trains, cops and robbers manifest within this opening.

Some teachers will tell you that the world of form is an illusion. Although this may be true, if you smash a brick against your head, it will hurt like hell. So, the teaching that all form is illusion does not account for the whole truth. It does not include the whole reality of life. Just as you get comfortable bathing in pure, delightful formlessness, form comes back to whack you over the head. It may come in the form of a brick or a terminal illness or it may come in the form of an insult hurled at you which cuts deeply into an unseen identification with some past psychological image of yourself. Let every experience happen. Every experience, thought, fear, hurt, pain, resentment, label, role, identity, and attachment is dying to die in the light of awareness. It is all One. So love comes back for everything, which means it comes back for itself.

The opening to which these words are pointing is Buddha's "Middle Way." It has no point of reference. The opening includes the whole truth. It is neither form nor pure awareness. To even make a distinction between those two and pretend that one or the other is the whole truth is . . . well . . . false. The whole devours all your attempts to hide within a part of it. Every bit of the false wants to come up and be swallowed by the truth. So, "cooperate with the inevitable," as Anthony De Mello put it.

A Zen master will tell his pupil not to get stuck in duality or non-duality. To what is he referring? Well, we can use all sorts of words that point to the opening: alert, present, aware, silent, peaceful, empty, spacious. Those are wonderful words, and they are especially helpful in leading you to see that you are not a thing or a process as Heidegger says. But non-alertness, thought, noise, non-peace, non-spaciousness, and all other forms appear and disappear inseparably within and through this silent, immovable opening. A nuclear bomb is inseparable from silence itself.

You are neither space nor matter.

Neither awareness nor thought.

Neither silence nor sound.

Neither formlessness nor form.

Neither peace nor non-peace.

Perhaps just ask whether you absolutely know that you are any of these things or no things, whether there is any distinction at all between them, and whether there is a you there to know any of that. If you are fixating on any aspect of reality, you are creating separation between your point of fixation and its opposite, and therefore have not realized your true nature as the opening. You are attached to a dream. Yes, it is true that the word silence points to our true nature. But this silence is beyond anything the mind can grasp. It has nothing to do with the letters s-i-l-e-n-c-e. The word is merely a symbol. If you believe with your mind that you are silence, you will wonder where the silence went when noisy thought arises. Do not seek the silence when noise is appearing or vice versa. That is just a continuation of the spiritual search.

The word "opening" is being used here not to create another concept apart from awareness or Oneness, but rather as a simple pointer: don't become fixated on any thing or no-thing that is arising or not arising. But if fixation arises, notice it. The opening is simply open to what is. Seeking, fixating, and escaping are devoured in that openness. When there is complete presence to what is arising, there is a realization that you are not only the opening, but also what arises within it. Another way of saying it is that all there is, is 'This.'

The Junkie and the Guru Within

Talk to a heroin junkie. He will tell you that drugs are a means of escaping the reality of now. The junkie gets a fix, but is always looking for the next or better dope. Spirituality can become a drug. Instead of heroin, the drug is some future moment where the seeker believes he will find perfect emptiness, awareness, Oneness, presence, enlightenment, liberation, the fulfillment of some belief system, or union with God. As Adyashanti says, reality is "perfect unity free of all reference points, with nowhere to stand and nothing to grab hold of." Mature spirituality is being at one with the ever-changing reality of this moment in whatever form it takes. It is no longer running from fear or trying to escape into some comfort zone or future ideal. It is no longer fixating on what you have and no longer looking for what you do not have. It is no longer buying into the illusion that there is a separate self to have or not have anything. When you escape into or go searching for an idea, state, belief, or other fragment, you shut out the whole. You shut out the truth.

Once awakening occurs, joy arises. Liberation from attachment to form naturally brings joy. Do you notice a sense of joy within? Maybe it is a subtle tingling sensation in your body or a sense that you are free-falling through space. Wonderful. Enjoy it. But realize that joy is a by-product of the opening. The opening is that within which this by-product arises. If you do not see this clearly, you will be much like the heroin junkie, fixated on the by-product, looking for his next fix, wondering where the joy went when confusion or pain arises within the opening. The truth is a moment bathing in pure loving beingness and a brick to the head—all the same.

One particularly clear expression of the opening is Buddha's "no self." This is nice because it expresses the realization that fixation happens because the mind perceives a center. This center is what becomes fixated on a characterization, a by-product, or some reference point along the way. With the realization that there is no you as a thought-based separate identity the center goes away. But watch thought come back in and try to define who you are. The junkie is back. He is seeking another point of reference, another self-definition, another center. You may then find yourself saying that you are liberation, simplicity, presence, One, formlessness, the universe, life, enlightenment, awareness, a child of God, or no self. That is fine. Don't vilify or condemn the use of these characterizations, just hold them lightly. The words, "You are the unnamable opening," are held lightly. This book—with all its concepts—is like a handful of flour. I blow into my palm. It shoots out into the air as a white cloud. The cloud illustrates that the flour and air are one. Then it falls away. Nothing left. No fixation. No center. To get stuck on any fragment is to obscure this truth that "cannot be expressed" or grasped through thought no matter how pointed the words are.

Are you free from wanting to be free, with nothing to grab onto? If not, you are fixating on some fragment within the whole. The fragment cannot see the whole.

Once the mind no longer gets stuck in identification with the various concepts used to point to the truth, such as formlessness, Oneness, presence, or enlightenment, all or any of these words can be used without making a problem out of any of them. A great way to notice where you are stuck is to watch what happens when someone disagrees with you as you attempt to teach him that he is not a separate person, that he is formlessness, or that it is all One. Perhaps he is a Christian or a Hindu and he strongly disagrees with your characterization of who he is or what the truth is. Watch the reaction within you. Do you feel the energy of insistence rising up because you see him as ignorant? You are now the spiritual ego, just another idea battling for supremacy against other ideas (e.g., Christianity, Hinduism) in the world of form.

But do not make a problem out of that. Realize the opening in which the insisting and battling take place.

No matter how enlightened you feel, the Christian or Hindu is now your teacher. But if you look a little closer, you see that the insistence energy within is your true teacher. This is the guru within. Whereas the junkie is always chasing the truth or believing it has attained it, the guru within is showing you that the whole movement of chasing and attaining is an illusion. The guru is telling you exactly where you are stuck. It tells you who you think you are despite your insistence that you are not identified with anything. It is always pointing to your true nature as the unnamable opening. That is what the truth does. It devours what is false.

Twenty-four
LIBERATION

What is the master [within you] who at this very moment is seeing and hearing? If you reply, as most do, that it is Mind or Nature or Buddha or one's Face before birth or one's Original Home or Koan or Being or Nothingness or Emptiness or Form... or the Known or the Unknown or Truth or Delusion, or say something or remain silent, or regard it as Enlightenment or Ignorance, you fall into error at once.

— Huang Po

People come here with some profound concept of spirituality. They think they have spiritual knowledge and they want me to give them a clean certificate. This I don't do. I blast their concepts... All knowledge is ignorance.

— Nisargadatta Maharaj

The only true wisdom is in knowing you know nothing.

— Socrates

You can't follow a spiritual path like a lemming to enlightenment. It simply doesn't work that way. An unwillingness to question every step of the way will stop you dead in your tracks. The path to enlightenment is strewn with those who have chosen to take a position or an identity along the way. And the closer you get to enlightenment the more dead bodies you will be stepping over until finally you step right out of yourself and arrive at the goal, exactly where you have always been. Except now there is no one standing there.

— Adyashanti

Holding beliefs or emphasizing thoughts such as, "It's all One," or "there is no self," does not constitute enlightenment. These are merely ideas. They are great pointers, but the mind can easily believe that the truth is *in the words.* Even mental positions about silence, awareness, and other pointers can be obstacles. They can actually keep thought locked into the dream of self. Belief cannot see 'This' because belief is identification with thought. And identification with thought *is* ego. Maybe the simplest definition of ego is that movement within you that indulges and emphasizes thoughts, making them into beliefs. Belief is all about maintaining a personal identity as the one who believes or holding a mental position as the one who knows. When you are interested only in protecting and building your positions and beliefs, you cannot know the freedom beyond all positions and beliefs. This freedom is available only when you let each thought pass right by, like a breeze blowing through the air. That includes your thoughts about spirituality or freedom itself. 'This' just is. It is free, loving, and open. It has no preference for the characterizations we place on it, the positions we take on it, or the identities we make out of it. Thought is temporary, self-involved, and largely involuntary. To believe that thought can truly tell you who you are or what 'This' or God is, is the dream.

What Is 'This'?

So what is 'This?' What is enlightenment? It is not the words 'This,' One, enlightenment or God. 'This' is realized through seeing what it is not. Liberation is beyond belief and thought, and yet it includes it. In other words, it plays with preferences and concepts, but it is not attached to them. It is not seeking a sense of self from them. True liberation is liberated from caring about characterizations about it, including the characterization "liberation." No wonder Jesus spoke in parables. The ultimate truth cannot be expressed. Every word and concept is a parable, no matter how precisely it is pointing to the truth.

This is equally "true" of non-duality or Oneness as it is sometimes called. If you listen to non-duality teachers or read books on it, the mind may start to believe this stuff. It gets lost again in the conceptual. Then, it believes that all is One. But belief will never see 'This.' 'This' is nothing the intellect can grasp. It is vast, and includes it all. 'This' does not get stuck on the level of the mind in any way, including notions that we should use only certain words or that words can even express it. In other words, 'This' does not get stuck on self. 'This' is that within which expressions of 'This' arise.

To say that the spirit should be expressed a certain way, or is a certain thing, comes from a point of reference, which is identification with thought. It is self. If I use the word "God" or "Allah" here and you are a Christian or a Muslim, something in your brain will register that word as being the truth. On the other hand, if you read a lot of non-duality books, the word "One" or "presence" may trigger a familiar mental response. The brain is simply stuck in words and beliefs. It is chasing after its own ideas. This stuckness is obscuring the truth of 'This.'

Enlightenment is not an affirmative belief. It is a project of removal—the negation of all that is not absolutely true. How does one negate what is false? He does not. Only thought would seek to do something like that. The false falls away naturally when awareness notices the dream self in each moment in each of its manifestations. What is left after that falling away is the unnamable, loving depth of truth itself. What is left is 'This.' The Divine.

Liberation Is No Self

Liberation has no point of reference. It has no center. That is "no self." This is why it can love fully, deeply, and freely all that is. Liberation simply watches. It notices. It sees all points of reference. It sees the brain's stuckness. It realizes that it is not any particular point of reference within its field of awareness. It is that which is looking at all points. In that realization, consciousness disentangles from its messy attachment to thought, from its illusion as a separate self. It is realized that the entire world is a dream being reflected by the mind. Thus, it is seen that any true transformation of this world must come from within, where the delusion lies.

When someone says, "Hey, look at this piece of paper," I do not really believe it is a piece of paper. Or better yet, I do not know what it is. I go along with it for practical purposes, but I feel I should sort of wink at the person, or nudge her a little, as if to say, "You don't really believe this is paper, do you?" No matter how many people agree to call this paper, that does not make it paper. Words are not that which they describe.

I am not trying to be clever or cute. I do not know with any mental certainty if 'This' is awareness, Oneness, aloneness, enlightenment, presence or God. Meister Eckhart expressed this clearly:

> *No idea represents or signifies itself. It always points to something else, of which it is a symbol. And since man has no ideas, except those abstracted from external things through the senses, he cannot be blessed by an idea.*

Thus, for purposes of communication, this is paper and that is a pencil. For purposes of spiritual teachings, "awareness" is a great pointer. But these words seem to imply that there is such a thing as mental certainty or that man can be blessed by an idea. Is that what 'This' is? Is this awareness? Is this Oneness? Is this God? Those are ideas. For purposes of this book, these ideas have been used to describe the indescribable.

But let's not fool each other about the real truth. The real truth is "I don't know." Not knowing is a fact. It is not a belief or a thought. But even that does not matter. To whom does it matter? It matters only to a thought, a mental self that is seeking something from it. The mind just wants to hold onto something, doesn't it? It wants to be someone in relation to others (better, worse, sadder, more unfortunate, richer, more knowledgeable, more spiritual, more enlightened). But life is impermanent and ever-changing. Any attempt to hold onto something causes suffering and conflict. The truth will continue to destroy your illusion that you somehow know who you are or what God is or what life means until you completely surrender to the truth of not knowing. Love absolutely flourishes in that unknowing. Love takes its rightful place as the truth when all the mental grasping towards the truth dies.

You may hang onto the notion that you are a certain role you are playing such as victim, mother, father, son, daughter, engineer, scientist, spiritual teacher, spiritual seeker, cancer survivor, recovering addict, doctor, or secretary. But none of it is you, and none of it is true. In fact, these self-images are remnants of the past keeping you stuck in thoughts about yourself. They constitute the dream of self-centeredness. Whether you realize it or not, you are looking for life circumstances to confirm what you already think you know about yourself and life. That search obscures the love that is who you truly are.

The phrase "I don't know" may sound idiotic to the mind that is identified with thought. To a spiritual seeker with some mental accumulation of non-duality teachings, "I don't know" may sound enlightened. But "I don't know" is not inherently anything. Thought will see "I don't know" from whatever perspective strengthens its point of reference. What is it that has jumped off the words "I don't know" and is free-falling? That is 'This.' Liberation. True love. The mind will do anything to avoid free-falling in the true "I don't knowness" of it all. Yet once it starts the free-fall, it knows unmistakably that it is in the truth. In some way that is inexplicable, realizing the state of mentally not knowing allows everything to be known through the heart, a level much deeper than the mind can grasp.

If you have a point of reference, you are not free-falling. If you are mentally certain about anything, you are not in the truth. If you believe you are awareness or a child of God, I have some swamp land at the North Pole to sell you. If I believe that anything that has been said in this book is the actual truth, then you can sell that swamp land back to me. If we believe that there is a separate you and me here to have, know, believe, agree or disagree about any of these things, we ought to invest in that land together. We can call it dreamland.

Presence is a wonderful word because when presence is fully here, thought subsides, and when it arises, it is not seen as a problem. Presence is liberation from identification with thought. The cessation of attachment to thought then shows you that all is One. It shows you God. It shows you that you, a child, and God are not separate. You are the chair, the house, and the road too. Yet, in a way that the conceptual mind cannot grasp, 'This' includes it all. It includes the dream of separation between apparent things. It includes words. It includes the use of words like "we" or "me" or "you." It includes the characterization "child of God." But the real truth of who you are knows that the words are not the ultimate truth. They are merely arising within it. Even if a certain way of expressing spirit is sharper than another way, in order to realize 'This' all pointers must be seen as not ultimately true. The concepts can obscure this truth that is so intimately and inescapably close and simple as the very life that *is* in this moment. As Jeff Foster states, the truth is immediately accessible as the "utterly, utterly obvious" simplicity of what is.

The words One and God are not the ultimate truth. They point to it. Once this ultimate truth is realized fully, those words lose whatever heavy meaning they carry in the dream state.

Have you made an issue out of the concepts "One" or "non-duality?"

Have you made an issue out of the concepts "awareness" or "formlessness?"

Have you made an issue out of the concepts "you, "me," or "we?"

Have you made an issue out of the concept "God?"

Have you made an issue out of the concepts "religion," "my religion," "your religion," or "their religion?"

Have you made an issue out of the concepts "self" or "no self?"

Have you made an issue out of the concepts "thought" or "presence?"

Have you made an issue out of the concept 'This?'

There is no issue. It is all a dream. Man cannot be blessed by an idea. When there is an issue or problem in your mind, thought is simply stuck in the notion that thought knows something or that it is in control. It does not and it is not. Thought only knows whatever it makes important. The dream self will create fundamentalism out of any concept, not realizing that there is nothing to hold onto. There is only 'This.' To create a point of reference and then look for others to agree or disagree with that point, no matter how "enlightened" the point appears, just strengthens the dream of self-centeredness and separation. When you have a point of reference, you are holding onto a fragment of 'This.' You are the false masquerading as the truth.

Identification with thought is the reason why humans have been disagreeing over God for centuries. They are not disagreeing over that to which the word God points. That to which it points is untouched by our little conceptual disagreements. Thought is simply disagreeing with thought. One dream self separating itself from another. Because consciousness is identified with thought, there is an appearance of people disagreeing, which turns to groups, nations, and religions disagreeing, which turns to conflict and war. All of that comes from a fundamental misunderstanding of who we are at the deepest level. One could say "beingness" or "Oneness" or "love" if those words are not held too tightly. The word is not the thing it describes. That cannot be said enough.

'This' cannot be named with any mental certainty. We simply cannot know the truth with any mental certainty. The words of this book are pointing away from themselves to a place of no reference points. That is not to make yet another point of reference, but rather to say: Do you see that which is closer than anything we can say about it? Do you realize yourself as life itself?

Do you realize that beingness simply is? You simply are, prior to any thought, idea, description, insistence or characterization, and prior to your conception of being a self or no self or having a religion or no religion.

The highest truth is not knowing. That is "no self." To the conceptual mind that may sound scary or nonsensical. But it is the highest truth. Awakening reveals a higher spiritual intelligence that has always been here, because it is all there is. It is not higher as in "better," but higher as in free from the bondage of seeking or attaching to notions of better vs. worse, or higher vs. lower. It is that within which the entire law of opposites is playing out. Yet only thought would label something higher or lower, better or worse. The highest truth is liberated from believing that it is the highest truth. Meister Eckhart expressed this beautifully: "God expects but one thing of you, and that is that you should come out of yourself in so far as you are a created being made and let God be God in you." Eckhart was speaking of humility. Letting God be God in you simply means allowing this preoccupation with a separate self and its attainment or non-attainment to die so that the peace of God can be realized through the body and mind.

Spirit does not seek itself. It is already whole and here in this moment. Only thought chases spirit, not realizing that attachment to thought itself is obscuring the recognition of spirit. Humanity has been searching for spirit not realizing that we already are that. The whole notion of spiritual seeking could be summed up this way: thought that believes thought holds the truth and then sets out to find it or believes it has it.

Living the One

Many understand the drop merging into the ocean but few understand the ocean merging into the drop.

— *Kabir*

There is a vast difference between believing in God or having a conceptual understanding of Oneness *and* living as that truth moment by moment. With just a little spiritual reading or work, the ego tends to get stuck. The intellect identifies with spiritual concepts. The spiritual ego is born. It believes it knows something and is more spiritual than others or it believes it lacks something and is less spiritual than others. There is no such thing as more or less spiritual. There is only spirit. Thought simply gets stuck again in the dream of self. The spiritual ego may then set out to debate and argue with others about spirituality in order to confirm its identity, knowledge or positions. When the intellect points outward to the other insisting that the other's conception of the truth is not correct, the intellect is face down, stuck in the mud of the conceptual. In the matter of the spirit, the intellect is deaf, blind, and dumb. The ultimate teaching of non-duality is the jumping off of all conceptual points into that which is prior to and inclusive of all points. The word non-duality points to liberation itself, including liberation from all belief systems and all concepts. Yet liberation plays with any and all points, concepts, and beliefs— deriving no sense of self from the playing. This truth is so inexpressible, yet so exquisitely true once it is realized.

To embody Oneness means to embody love in each moment, which just means to realize that you are that love and that nothing is separate from it. Thus, all your arguments, disagreements, and ideas about the truth are arising within a dream of self. Your behavior towards others and the way you move through the world are revealing everything about how deep the realization of Oneness has gone within your body and mind. This is what Kabir meant by the ocean merging into the drop. For example, you know you are identified with the concept of Oneness (rather than living as the reality of it) when you believe Christians are ignorant or Scientologists are foolish or when you insist that your description of enlightenment is the right one. As a Christian, you know you are identified with the thought of God (rather than living in the truth of God) when you find yourself arguing with a Buddhist, or someone who says, "All is One." There are not two truths—the mind is simply fragmented. A fragment cannot see the whole. It is only interested in maintaining itself—its own religion, belief system, or path. That is the nature of self-centeredness.

Spiritual disagreement is a maddening game of self-centered delusion. 'This' simply is, beyond the egoing that likes to sink its claws into the concepts of 'This.' The deepest truth of beingness is liberated from attachment to conceptual expressions of itself. Only a dream self who is seeking to be, or know, or become something in relation to someone else would care about trying to win at this illusory game. In the game of humility, love is the grand prize. You can never win the prize because it is only awarded in your absence. But when the self is realized to be the dream it is, there is only love. Everyone wins.

The spirit does not disagree, only thoughts do. Holy wars are spiritual searches. They take many forms. They do not always result in physical violence. Sometimes they arise as a disagreement in a Sangha, spiritual center, twelve-step meeting or church about how the truth should be characterized, what God's will is, or what enlightenment is. These disagreements are about the self. They are not about the truth. This does not mean that you should not express your opinions. It means do not believe for one minute that your point is the objective truth or that thought can grasp 'This.' Your point is merely a perspective. It is a dream. Have fun in the dream. Play in it. Liberation plays. It is not authoritative or argumentative. It does not know. Liberation is wise and loving, not because it has accumulated fancy points of reference or because it has settled into correct beliefs about wisdom or love. It is wise because it is ultimately free of all points and is therefore naturally in love with the whole.

A holy war does not begin with a gun. It is born when consciousness identifies with a past spiritual insight. Any organization organized around a belief system that separates those who follow it from those who do not is enslavement to an idea, to a fragment. It is a weapon of separation. No religion or belief system can be created from genuine spiritual insight. The only "thing" which would ever try to carry an insight forward is a dream self, intent on identifying with a particular idea in order to separate itself from the illusory others who "don't get it" or "don't believe it." True insight is constantly revealing that all is One and therefore that divisions are false.

You find God when you stop dreaming about him and stop trying to convince yourself and others that he does or does not exist, or that you have found him or will find him. You realize that God is only ever here, right here, in this moment. The spiritual search ends when it is realized that you could not possibly improve upon this immovable, unchanging spirit within you. The only thing that would ever measure "improvement" is a temporary thought moving through this spirit.

The expressions "no self," "no center," and "no point of reference" include not making the One or God your mental point of reference. To be full of ideas is to be empty of God. To be empty of ideas is to be full of God. The moment you are attached to or identified with the concept that there is only One Life or that there is a God or that there is no self, you become the dream self—the separation. You are then conflict. You are the holy war, despite your insistence on your own holiness. If the thought arises that you are enlightened, present, a child of God, or liberated, or that you have spiritual knowledge, let it arise. Just notice it. None of it is true, and none of it is you. There is no self to be or know any of those things. There is only this spirit. 'This.'

The liberation of not knowing is an emptiness that is filled by the divine. Your attachment to ideas about the divine leaves no emptiness for the divine to fill. Once you become an idea, you begin separating yourself from others who do not believe it and from the divine which is the source of it. In liberation, ideas and concepts do not go away. Liberation does not make an enemy out of the intellect. This is why Huang Po stated that it is error to call this freedom the known or the unknown. In liberation, even the intellect is seen to be a perfect expression of spirit. To reject the intellect would be to reject form, and therefore to reject spirit itself. But liberation uses ideas and concepts in the service of love (i.e., the divine), rather than in service to the dream self.

Do you see the madness yet? 'This' is prior to, beyond, and inclusive of all these characterizations such as One, 'This,' or God. Once that is realized, we are playing in the truth like children. The truth is simply free, including free from any notion that we can truly communicate it. It is free to use knowledge as a helpful map to point to and conceptualize about 'This' without ever confusing the map with the reality to which it is pointing. It is free to allow words and thoughts to flow freely, without making the words into an identity or a position. We are free to use the words "we," "you," and "me" without any concern that those words in any way take us out of the realization of Oneness. They cannot. If we built pronouns the size of skyscrapers, we would still be in 'This.' We cannot escape 'This.' If you are wondering what 'This' is still, notice the cognizing space within which the wondering arises. That is 'This.' Paradoxically, everything that arises within 'This' is also 'This." Non-duality. Oneness. Inseparability. Love. That is what these words are pointing to. Just look. Be free. Live without divisions. If you still have any division between a 'this' and a 'that,' you don't have love. You have separation.

Love's Revolution

When you are free of all fixed mental positions, there is no longer a separate "you." There is only love. Everything in life . . . every thought, emotion, state, experience, event, and object . . . is seen to be like a breeze that passes through air. The air and the breeze are One. They are inseparable. At first, it may seem as if you are the air only. It may seem as if thought happens WITHIN you. But even THAT is seen to be a subtle mental position in the end. It is just another division of the mind. To stand apart from something is still duality. It may even be detachment or even apathy. This is not about detachment. This is perfect love. Non-duality.

This book is not ultimately about awareness, if the word "awareness" is pointing to a witness that stands somehow apart from what is being witnessed. Don't believe the Gurus that tell you that you are awareness. It's just another religion. Use the pointer "awareness" as a tool only. Let it show you that everything seems to arise in awareness. Let it show you that it APPEARS like you are awareness. Then let that duality between awareness and what appears within awareness collapse. Be free of that division.

When you really believe you are awareness, notice that you still have a subtle mental position. Let it drop away completely. See that, when a thought arises, it has no independent existence from the awareness that sees it. It is like a cloud of steam that arises in space. The steam and the space are inseparable. They are "not two."

Go look for the line between awareness and the things that happen within awareness. Every time you think you have found a line, see that you have found only another thought. Thought creates the appearance of divisions. It is only an appearance. In that seeing, all that is left is love. This is love's revolution. Self and other are inseparable. Iran and America are inseparable. Christian and Muslim are inseparable. Democrat and Republican are inseparable. Awareness and appearances are inseparable. Form is none other than emptiness and emptiness is none other than form. These "things" appear together, in an inseparable dance. They do not exist alone, apart from one another. When one arises, the other arises with it. The line between these things is conceptual only. When you see that the viewpoint you reject completely is inseparable from you, all conflict is seen through. What is left is love.

This message is not a life-denying or world-denying message. It is not a concept-denying message either. Concepts are seen to be beautiful and perfect when you realize they are not really pointing to separate things at all. When that is seen, you are free to think or not think. It just doesn't matter anymore. Would freedom look any other way?

This message is not a mental position about seeing through all divisions. It is not a position. It is pointing you out of being stuck in positions. This is about a seeing. It is a celebration of this world, with all its perspectives. It is ultimately a celebration of diversity itself. It is a celebration of duality. The line between non-duality and duality is also just a conceptual line. In seeing through that, you cannot know that you are a self or not a self. You cannot know that nothing exists or that everything exists separately. You can only be whatever you are, in whatever way that appears. Look around. Everything is appearing and disappearing in a constant flow of change. You are THAT. This is freedom from all dualistic extremes. This is what it means to live life in a completely undivided and loving way.

You will know non-dual realization when it dawns on you. You will close this book and never open it again. I wrote this book knowing that if you realize the truth to which it points, you will stop reading it. When liberation strikes, you will see your favorite guru as no different than your neighbor or a frog beside the road. You will stop being concerned with making the point that your guru, your neighbor, and the frog are not separate. You will know in your heart that they are not separate, but you will see that the mental insistence energy behind your point just creates the illusory separate self known as you. You will stop making points about God as if you have any idea who or what that is. Or you will continue making points without any notion that your points have anything to do with that to which the word God points. You will realize that you are the truth and will have little use for books like this that only point to it.

You will stop placing egoic projections on teachers and stop believing they have something you do not. You will love your fellow man and the frog beside the road infinitely more than ever before, not because some book told you to or because you believe that you are love or that this is what God wants for you. You will realize yourself as love and will see yourself in your fellow man and the frog. But if you believe what I have said too early, you will simply enter a delusion about Oneness, a belief about this truth, which will separate you from those who do not believe it. Belief makes points about the truth. This book makes points. The truth simply is.

If all non-duality and enlightenment teachers and teachings disappear into obscurity, love will have realized itself fully. Non-duality is the only message for which there are no return visitors. The truth burns everything that is false including teachers and teachings. When consciousness is liberated from identification with form, the spirit is realized to be love itself. Love realizes itself as this One. It loves fully all that it sees. It wants to free and be free because it is—at its core level—already free. It does not love partially. It does not create new religions out of anything said here or anywhere. It does not shed blood through a holy war. It does not point outward to the other in negative judgment. It does not get stuck on any point of reference, whether it is a point about what God is or a point about how others should not behave the way they do.

Love does not argue with the reality of what is. It is at peace with that reality. It sees reality as itself. It acts without expectation of reward or any return on its investment. It does not care about being right or gaining an advantage through its actions. It speaks and acts clearly and sometimes forcefully but always without an inkling that it has any control.

You already are liberation. More pointedly, there is no one there to be liberated. A story of becoming has been obscuring this realization. If you have hope for liberation in the future, you do not see that hope is simply a presently-arising thought, which gives you more time and therefore more searching, which means more self. The concept of "hope" is standing in the way of liberation. Liberation is only now. Hope is a figment of the mind that is not at one with life in this moment. If you realized yourself as happiness now and that there is no way you could ever be separate from it, you would have no need for the word "hope." Enlightenment is radical. It changes everything. It is surrendering the entire dream self to the liberation of 'This.' 'This' is the present moment. The dream of hope is a dream of tomorrow, which means a dream that is constantly leading you away from 'This.' In the realization of 'This,' life continues to unfold and the purpose for which you are here is realized, but there is no separate self seeking to gain anything from that unfolding. The whole (God, if you prefer) is taking action through you.

Fear is just the flipside of hope. Both fear and hope are illusory attempts to escape life in this moment. Behind every thought of hope for the future, there is a subtle, underlying fear that the future will not fulfill you. The concept of "hope" would not even arise without that underlying dissatisfaction of this moment and fear of future. Behind every thought of fear towards the future, there is a subtle desire or hope that the future will not be as bad as your dream suggests. Face these illusory movements called hope and fear the moment they arise. They are ghosts—mirages. They obscure the fullness of life now. When the dream self dissolves, both hope and fear dissolve with it because they were illusions from the start. Love remains because it is not an illusion.

Do not place your happiness in time, in the dream. Any thought you have of where your mind-made spiritual path will end up is your own projection. It is your thought, your memory, what you have learned, projecting itself forward. This is the loop of self-centeredness. If you are chasing your own projection, you will only ever meet that projection. You will only ever meet your own memory. True liberation is unrecognizable. It does not arise from memory. It is that which is aware of how your memory is imprisoning you in self-centeredness. True love exists outside of this dream self.

To liberation, liberation of the personal self does not matter anymore. There is no longer a separate self seeking liberation. A self can never find liberation anyway. Unconditional love and liberation are only realized when the dream of a thought-based self is dissolved. The moment the self seeks liberation as a thought-based future dream, it is in bondage. Do not try to suppress thought. Only thought would do that. Simply allow whatever is arising. In that allowing, it is realized that liberation was always and already here under all the grasping and seeking. Do not make liberation into a future goal. The mind will make a goal out of anything, which just keeps the self and the search alive. It will make a goal out of enlightenment, self, no self, thought, no thought, Oneness, love, presence, inquiry, God, or liberation. The goal stands in the way of liberation. The goal is the self, the fragment, the point, the dream, the obstacle to the timeless God.

In the realization of the ground of beingness in the present moment, the separate self is transcended. Then life continues to unfold. Becoming happens. But it is not ego caught in the trap of self-seeking anymore. Instead, it is Oneness being embodied in the human form. True enlightenment is no longer being lost in personal goals, achievements, titles, roles, paths, beliefs, positions, and identities. In enlightenment, there is still a conventional self, like a fiction, but that self is in no way separate from the rest of life. Any becoming is no longer tied to the idea that a self can (or would even desire to) gain anything from the becoming. When the self is gone, nothing feels like it is missing. The insanity of personal becoming and personal seeking that is the hallmark of the dream self is replaced with completeness. All stories of becoming, evolving, and changing are fine and wonderful when nothing feels lost or missing on a personal level. One sees that it is impossible to add anything to completeness yet, paradoxically, nothing stops one from moving to bring about apparent change in life. In short, love becomes fully embodied in humanness (i.e., the ocean merges into the drop). Life is a celebration. One is finally able to live life without the fear embedded in the belief of being a separate self. This living includes allowing life to unfold within a story. Yet there is no longer attachment to ideas about how that story should play itself out. Even the story of self is Oneness.

So how is this love and freedom realized? It is already here, in this moment, underneath the energy of the dream self that is locked into a search for the next moment. It is right where you are right now. It is what is looking. It is watching each sight, listening to each sound, smelling each smell, and breathing each breath. It is that which sees that all suffering is a dream of self and then reaches out to help another see it. It is the smell of hot cinnamon rolls, the sound of your friend's voice, footsteps walking up to your door, a lonely weed in your garden, raindrops on your forehead, the bright sun warming your arms, a bird perched on a roof, the freezing cold of snow and ice, the sound of people arguing, and the flushing of a toilet. It is stroking the cat, napping on the couch, washing your car, shopping for groceries, watching the thought, feeling the feeling, and noticing your inattention to these things. It is being at one with whatever is arising, realizing that only love is ever arising and that there is no one here seeking anything from it.

Every moment is teaching us. But it is not teaching us an accumulation of ideas, which we can carry with us over time. We are not becoming spiritual egos who know something. Life is teaching us that we are not separate from it and that love means not knowing, not resisting, and not trying to control. Accumulation, by its very nature, creates a rigid, separate dream self which is trying to know, resist, and control life. This self is at war with life.

Insight is fresh, new, innocent, and clear. It cannot be carried over into the next moment. True spiritual learning has nothing to do with memory. It is the moment by moment awareness of what is arising and falling. It is holding onto nothing. It is the wisdom that sees that life begins and ends in this moment. It is constantly waking you up out of your points of reference, out of your false sense of mental certainty, and out of the dream of separation—all of which is the past in you.

Love is asking to realize itself in each moment. All you have to do is notice the asking. Notice that you are the asking. Love does not exist in time—in the mind. It is not dependant on what happened, what is happening now, or what will happen. Only you, the dream self, are dependant. Love has no conditions and no agenda. It simply is. It simply loves.

The truth is love itself. Love knows that these words are not the truth. Love is what is looking out of those eyes and what sees these words. Searching and suffering end whenyou stop telling lies and stories, when you stop living life through beliefs and when you notice the love that isaware of these lies, stories, and beliefs. The truth has nothing to do with replacing one story with another story or one belief with another belief. It is not found whenyou go from telling a negative story to a positive story. Negative and positive are only relative truths arising within 'This.'

There is a deeper truth that is who you are beyond the story of self. This deeper truth is what sees the play between positive and negative. It sees everything and it is everything. Thus, it sees only itself. It cannot be named because it is that which is looking at all naming and storytelling. It is prior to all forms, stories, names, ideas, beliefs and selves. It includes and embraces those things without attachment to any of it. It appears inseparably as those things. Nothing is being everything. That is about as close as words can get.

Who would have known that, under all the seeking, who you truly are is love itself and that love is all there is, which is just another way of saying that God is all there is? They don't teach us that in school. To search for what is always and already here is insane. Enlightenment is your birthright because it is who you truly are under all these complicated stories of knowledge, becoming, and self.

The points of reference in this book are dead and of the past. They are of "Scott." Scott is a dream teacher who writes dream teachings about past spiritual insights. "Scott" and the insights in this book arise within 'This.' This book is playing in the liberation of love. If you do not see this or if you are arguing with "Scott" or this book, thought is simply stuck in a point of reference—a belief system that is strengthening a dream self.

There is no person here or anywhere else with whom to disagree, argue, or fight. Your conflict with others exists only within your own mental dream in which the reality of what is arising now does not match your stored memory and expectations. There is no spiritual authority here or anywhere else. Authority does not play. It obscures love. It is too busy separating itself from the whole. Authority tells, concludes, argues, and gets stuck on points. It insists on its own conceptions of the truth. These are all illusions destroyed by the real truth. The real truth is that there is only love seeing itself everywhere. Love is who we are, now, beyond all of our points. Love is that which embraces all points of view. It is appearing as every point of view, even the one that rejects what is being said in this book.

Notes

1   Luke 17:21, King James Version
2   *Tao Te Ching*, A New English Version, Stephen Mitchell, Harper Perennial Modern Classics, 2006
3   *Tao Te Ching*, A New English Version, Stephen Mitchell, Harper Perennial Modern Classics, 2006
4   Luke 17:20-21, English Standard Version
5   Romans 12:2, New International Version

Other books by
Scott Kiloby

Reflections of the One Life: Daily Pointers to Enlightenment

Living Realization

Natural Rest: Finding Recovery Through Presence

CPSIA information can be obtained at www.ICGtesting.com
Printed in the USA
LVOW061728211111

255956LV00001B/177/P

9 781419 695780